THREE VICARS
TALKING

THREE VICARS TALKING

The book of the brilliant BBC Radio 4 series

Rev Richard Coles, Rev Kate Bottley,
Rev Giles Fraser

First published in Great Britain in 2020

Society for Promoting Christian Knowledge
36 Causton Street
London SW1P 4ST
www.spck.org.uk

Copyright © BBC 2020
Illustrations copyright © Josefina Schargorodsky

British Library Cataloguing-in-Publication Data
A catalogue record for this book is available from the British Library

ISBN 978–0–281–08468–5
eBook ISBN 978–0–281–08467–8

Typeset by Manila Typesetting Company
First printed in Great Britain by TJ Books Limited
Subsequently digitally printed in Great Britain

eBook by Manila Typesetting Company

Produced on paper from sustainable forests

Contents

Foreword

The idea for this series came at the Greenbelt Festival when our Three Vicars gathered to swap stories of the everyday experiences of being a priest in the Church of England. It was a rainy day, but the tent was not just crammed with people listening and laughing – there were people standing outside in the rain under umbrellas or with their hoods up, and the trio did more than talk. They had the place in uproar one minute, listening silently the next and wiping away tears before the end.

The same proved true in *Three Vicars Talking* for BBC Radio 4. Though they were all different in style and backgrounds, the thing that was most striking was that they were friends – and the trust between them meant there were moments of real connection and poignancy alongside the laughter. They could rib each other mercilessly, console each other when the stories turned serious, and share that most special of qualities in a public conversation: an understanding of what it is that makes their day job a vocation, a calling, and a service to others.

The three topics we initially chose for the radio series were the bedrock of their interaction with their parishioners and the wider population: the moments of hatch, match and dispatch, which mark the three great moments of anyone's life – birth, love and death – and their ceremonial and sacramental markers, the christening, the wedding and the funeral.

The first three recordings, in front of a small audience, were done at St Martin-in-the-Fields. The Revd Kate Bottley, Canon Giles Fraser and the Revd Richard Coles are all performers. They had been talked through the shape of the subject areas to cover but, in truth, once they were plugged in, it was a case of letting them go.

Take weddings, for instance. Giles admitted to being the grumpy one – he doesn't like wedding videos: 'I'm ag'in the video man' – and in past summers, with five weddings a day, brides who were late could lose hymns at a rate of one every five minutes they were over time. Richard's anecdotes were definitely a cut above – with posh London churches hosting extravaganzas where wedding gowns could reach £80K and military guards of honour provided a 'flash of cutlery'. Kate described her 'wedding tool belt' to cover every eventuality – a sewing kit, black socks, a spare pair of women's shoes, and so on. Thousands follow each of them on social media, but it was Rev Kate, after all, who became famous for her flash-mob wedding video with ten million hits. 'If I possibly can, I just like to say yes,' she said.

For the recording on funerals, the three well-known broadcasters combined gallows humour with pathos. Now and again they excitedly jumped in with the next anecdote, but the doyenne of radio reviewers, Gillian Reynolds, was right when she wrote: 'Each seems genuinely engaged with the others' experiences, all are funny, wise, thoughtful, occasionally confessional.' This certainly was a rare glimpse into a vicar's life, with all the absurdities and profundities side by side. We know, too, from listeners that the conversations were not only entertaining and poignant but deeply reassuring. These are people who know how to manage death while being familiar with the most challenging aspects of living.

The last two specials for Christmas and Easter were recorded together just before the start of Advent 2019. The first beautifully caught the atmosphere of the coming season and the disagreements over 'Away in a manger' epitomized the fault line between sentimentality and raw emotion. Kate told her own share of moving personal stories but she was more likely to gently admonish the two men for their 'bladders being near their eye' when both were variously moved to weep at the people who had taught them about the fragility and extraordinariness of the capacity for human love.

We knew that recording Easter at the same time as Christmas meant it would be a long time 'on the shelf', but we were confident they could make it work – after all, it was timeless, for the purpose of finding the meaning in Easter.

There was no way we could have known that the New Year would bring with it the start of a global pandemic. It was immediately clear it would be impossible to broadcast the last programme as it was. Tens of thousands of people had died. The tone of the programme – recorded pre-coronavirus – felt like something from another era. Also, more personally, just before Christmas, Richard had been widowed with the sad death of his partner David, who was also an Anglican priest. He had to record it again.

Lockdown started, and changed everyone's lives, including broadcasters'. The programme had to be recorded with the three vicars talking on video calls, each from their own home. Never daunted, producer Neil Morrow engineered an elaborate set-up with them feeding into a BBC studio in Salford. They also, individually, had to record themselves into their own smart phones to ensure better sound quality. Once uploaded, Neil expertly mixed them together.

But the quality of the conversation overshadowed the technical achievement. As I listened in, I knew that this was something very special. All the programmes had been special in their own way, but this was something else. It was something truly important. They were talking to the nation in a time of crisis. They spoke of how this year, for each of them personally, Easter would be different. Richard talked about how the parish had been 'fantastic at exercising its priestly ministry to me – rather than me exercising my priestly ministry to them'. Without her own church, Kate imagined being home with her family: 'This year it'll probably be mostly just us, huddled together in a room with the rumour of the resurrection, which has a lovely echo of the first Easter for me.' Giles described the moment when a priest signals the resurrection by lighting the candle in the darkness. He always worried, he confided, that the candle might go out, 'because the resurrection is absolutely everything that our faith is built upon . . . We say, "The Light of Christ" . . . is it really going to light ourselves up? But it does.' What all three agreed was that this year was more intense than any other time in their lives.

Then Richard talked about a particular day when he had gone alone to visit David's grave. He revealed that for him grief brings a focused perspective that allows you 'to see stuff in a way you haven't seen before . . . what that promise of new life really means'. When he ran out of words, silence followed. Kate wept. Then Giles spoke: 'Something so beautiful needs to be responded to with silence.'

Three Vicars Talking about Easter was the crowning glory of a five-part series of conversations that laid bare – in its moments of laughter and sorrow and profound emotion – something rare. It was three people united in an understanding of the nature of human relationship on all its different and complex levels. Their faith in God, their friendship with each other and with those they serve was crowned with this moment of almost unbearable poignancy. In the broadcast we left the silence where it was, to allow listeners, in the closing moments of the programme, to join our three priests as they wished each other 'Happy Easter' through tears of sadness and joy.

Throughout the series we had heard each of them speak of the privilege of their work with people who are often at their most vulnerable. But those who minister are vulnerable too. This series gave us all – broadcasters and listeners alike – a privileged insight into that.

Christine Morgan
Head of BBC Radio Religion and Ethics

Death

Broadcast on Monday 19 August 2019, at 11 a.m.

Presenters:	**RICHARD COLES**
	KATE BOTTLEY
	GILES FRASER
Producer:	**NEIL MORROW**
Series editor:	**CHRISTINE MORGAN**
Music:	**'Another One Bites the Dust' by Queen**

COLES Welcome to our new series of divine conversation with me, the Reverend Richard Coles, and my dog-collared, never dog-eared, Church of England colleagues – the Reverends Kate Bottley and Giles Fraser. Over the next three weeks we'll be musing on births, weddings and death. Those three great pillars of our job – the hatch, the match and the dispatch.

Dispatching is often the one, don't you find with clergy, that really gets the anecdotes kind of coming thick and fast . . .

BOTTLEY Ooh, I love a funeral.

COLES Why do we love funeral stories so much?

FRASER Well, I think we love funerals – love funerals is the wrong way of putting it – but funerals are the one thing that we can – we have a particular contribution to make. So, not only in terms of what it is that we believe, that's rather particularly important here, but also that we're not so afraid of pain and death. And we're unusual with regard to that we're not freaked by it. So, actually, we can talk to people who are dying; we've talked quite a lot to people who are dying. We can talk about their dying, which is – sometimes it's a very lonely business because everybody else is pretending that they're *not* dying. So, we have a particular contribution that we can make. And so, I think that actually there's something that you can add to a funeral, in a way that you probably don't – you're more an impresario when you're doing a wedding.

BOTTLEY It's the most useful I feel, doing a funeral. It's the thing I walk away from and go: I did some good there; I actually made a difference at that one; I was able to give you lyrics, a script, a tune, a framework to hang everything on.

COLES And the thing is – well, it's because we're not really on terms with death in the way our ancestors were, simply because it was a daily reality for them in a way. And it's the one fate we all share, the one thing we will all experience, and yet so exported beyond the margins of consciousness.

The other thing about it that's interesting is people go a bit mad, don't they, because they're ill prepared for it, because bereavement can be so terrible and grief can be so terrible, it goes off like a bomb. And what we can do is sort of know what we're doing, and that's really important, I think, when people are in grief.

FRASER There's a calmness about – that you can add to it and so forth. And as Kate says, there's a sort of pattern to it, not just a pattern to the liturgy but the liturgy also reflects something about a pattern to life itself. And so there's a way in which you can order and structure and calm and console, all at the same time.

BOTTLEY You can feel them just breathe a little bit easier . . .

FRASER Especially when . . .

BOTTLEY . . . the minute – the minute when you go, 'I'm so sorry about your mum. How are you doing?' You can just hear them go, 'Oh, it's going to be all right; this bit's

3

going to be all right' – because they won't organize that many funerals in their lifetime and we can help take care of that.

COLES I used to think – I've learnt most about priesthood at deathbeds, actually, deathbeds and funerals. Best lesson I ever learnt was to shut up, actually, because – often you're at a deathbed with someone and it might be someone who's maybe not been encouraged to speak much, who might have a rich story to tell that they've never told, and all of a sudden on a deathbed that comes to be really important for them. And I used to sort of help them along with a story, like a bossy interviewer, and very quickly, when someone said shut up, you stupid twat . . . [laughter] I kind of learnt not to because, actually, one of our jobs, especially then, is to hear and I don't mean just to let the sound go into our ears, but I mean to hear something that's really profoundly important.

FRASER And absorb, absorb some of their pain or their sense of fear. Then actually if you can absorb it, it's okay, it's sort of – this is going to be manageable if someone else isn't going to run away from it.

BOTTLEY But you have to be careful what you say. I did kill a woman once . . .

FRASER Oh my . . .

COLES And I think I killed someone once too.

BOTTLEY I've killed – I'm sure we've all killed people. We have, haven't we?

FRASER Maybe – how did you kill someone?

BOTTLEY So, I was sat with her – it was one of my first weeks in a parish – and the husband had phoned me up and said, 'Can you come and see my wife – she's not very well? She's not expected to die but she's non-communicative.' So, I went to visit this lady, lovely, and I got into the room and the lady was there and she'd not spoken for years, she was non-communicative. And he kind of went, 'I'll let you two chat.' So, I was sat with this woman and of course hearing's the last to go, so I held her hand and I said, 'You can go, you know, if you want. He'll be fine. He comes to see you every day. If you need to go, just go, it's fine.' Anyway, so I anointed her, I went, and then she wasn't expected – she wasn't poorly. Went home, got a phone call in the night – you'll never guess what's happened?

FRASER So, she decided to go?

BOTTLEY So, I was just like – oh, my word. But it's true . . .

FRASER You didn't kill her, Kate.

BOTTLEY No, I know, but – so, I exaggerated for comic effect, Giles. I think that's one of the reasons we're here. [*laughter*] It's that permission given, isn't it? And I think you're right about, you know, the whole kind of thing of sitting alongside people that are dying. I remember saying to one person, 'So, are you ready for it then?' And the family went [*intake of breath*], like that, because I was asking if they were ready to die, you know: 'Are you ready for it yet?' And the family went, 'Don't tell her; she doesn't know.' She's in a hospice. What do you think she thinks is going to happen? Do you know what I mean? She has terminal cancer, you know; she knows she's not . . . But they were so scared of actually saying. And the family came in and went, 'Are you ready for your pudding, Mother? She meant, are you ready for your pudding?' I really didn't mean, 'Are you ready for your pudding?'

COLES One of my favourite ones – I was seeing a woman who was dying, who was in hospital, and she was up on a ward – a private room, rather – up on a floor. And she was a very religious woman, she was very sweet and she had a very, kind of simple, touching faith. And she was talking a little bit and she talked about how she was looking forward to seeing Jesus and that heaven would open. And I was sitting talking to her, and then all of a sudden she looked out and she kind of looked past me and her face sort of lit up, and I thought, oh my goodness, it's the heavens opening. And then I heard a bang on the window. I looked round and there was a charity abseiler, there was a bloke – there was literally a bloke on a rope going past her window. [*laughter*]

BOTTLEY I went to visit my verger, who was dying, Maureen, and I went in and she'd got some quiz show on or something – because they put the telly on for people, don't they, because people are so scared of silence in that moment. So, the telly was on full blast, some sort of awful quiz show thing. So, I walked in and she was in the bed and I turned the TV over and went to sit with her and held her hand. She opened her eyes and she looked at me – and I leant in – and I went, 'It's all right Maureen, I'm here, love.' And she went, 'Can you put that on? I want to see if they win jackpot.' [*laughter*]

But the hospital visiting – I remember going up to visit a gentleman and it was my first death call. Do you remember your first phone call – 'Get here now'? It was my first one as a curate – 'He's going, get here now.' So, I legged it to the hospital, ran up to the ward, got to the ward, realized that I'd left the holy oils in the car, just went – I can't – all nervous, shaky, shaky, shaky. The family were there, they needed to see me do the thing, so that he could go. So, I ferreted in my handbag, found whatever I had to hand and said to God – this is going to have to do. So, I anointed the bloke with Clinique moisturizer cream. [*laughter*]

COLES That's posh.

BOTTLEY And he lived for another eight weeks. And I like to think when they laid him out, he had a beautifully moisturized cross on his forehead. But I did say to God – I will come back and do it properly; if he lives I . . .

FRASER Other moisturizers are available.

BOTTLEY Yeah, other moisturizers – I will come back and do it properly.

COLES Can I just admit to you that my first ever call-out, it was – I was just ordained as a deacon and it was to a nursing home. And I went to see a man – I can still remember his name – in a room at the end of a stairway, on his own, end of his life. And I went to anoint him and I made the sign of the cross on his forehead and he died.

BOTTLEY [*sharp intake of breath*]

COLES And I remember, he literally just opened his mouth and his last breath came.

BOTTLEY Wow.

COLES And I sort of went – ooh, err, err, what do I do, what do I do? I was sort of thrown by it.

FRASER That's very beautiful.

BOTTLEY Yeah, that's gorgeous.

COLES It was. He was a lovely man, great backstory, which I only found out about afterwards. But that felt like, you know, a blessing . . . But people do hang on, don't they? One of the most picturesque deaths I went to was a friend of mine who was a Roman Catholic priest who was dying. He was a priest in the Archdiocese of Westminster, the days when Cardinal Hume was the Archbishop. And he was laying and dying and we called the Cardinal and, being a cardinal, he said he was busy, but he said, 'I'll get there as soon as I can.' And he arrived at sort of end of the day and this guy had been struggling all the time. And so we left the Cardinal with the priest, and the Cardinal came out and said, 'He's gone.' And what had happened was he had gone in and he started to say the Gloria, but, typical Benedictine monk, he couldn't remember it in English so he did it in Latin instead. And the priest responded to that too and on the word 'Amen' just . . .

BOTTLEY Oh how gorgeous . . .

COLES Let go.

BOTTLEY . . . I'll take that now . . . Well, not now!

COLES But it does happen, doesn't it? The way people meet their death . . . and what we can be are the kind of people who help that encounter.

FRASER I had a heart attack and went into a quadruple heart bypass, and it was a major operation and I honestly thought that I'd . . . you know, you're not entirely sure that you'll survive it. And so I was being wheeled in the trolley down to theatre, and it so happened the porter who wheeled me was actually a member of my congregation, but this was entirely by chance. And so as I was chatting to him rather nicely I thought – the last thing I'm going to be doing in my life is going, 'Are you all right, mate? How are your kids, and what's happened to the dog?' and that sort of stuff. So, it was very mundane. I thought, is this going to be the last thing I ever say?

COLES But you get that, don't you, poetry and prose come together very closely.

BOTTLEY And of course, then there's the home visits when you get called to someone's home to anoint or to visit and the morphine driver's still going, and those kind of things. And there's that moment where they've died, and so they've called you over and you can still see the family photographs on the mantelpiece and the slippers and all that sort of stuff.

But my funeral director tells a story of when he got the phone call to come and collect. They arrived and of course the dispatch team came in with the trolley and the bag and everything, and the two sons were stood there and Dad's on the sofa, and with the two sons stood there they say, 'I'm sorry for your loss, I'm sorry for your loss.' And they say, 'This is going to take a few minutes, you might want to step outside or you might want to stay in the room.' 'No, we'll stay; no, we'll stay.' So, the funeral directors go over to Dad – ready to lift him in – and he coughs. And the two sons go, 'What are you *doing*? Mum's in't bedroom upstairs.' [*laughter*] And the funeral director said to me, 'I wouldn't mind but she looked better than he did.'

FRASER Oh undertakers, they're a whole programme . . .

BOTTLEY Oh, I love – I love an undertaker.

COLES I love them.

BOTTLEY I really fancy my undertaker, I really do.

COLES Of course, they are the professionals. Perhaps, apart from teachers, the ones with whom we spend most of our time, aren't they?

FRASER Yeah. I once got caught on Spaghetti Junction in Birmingham, lost in the hearse with a coffin in the back. And I don't know if you know Spaghetti Junction but it's absolutely impossible. And we were running . . .

BOTTLEY Going round and round.

FRASER ... going around Spaghetti Junction. We were about forty minutes going around Spaghetti Junction not being able to get off with the coffin ...

BOTTLEY Not all funeral directors are good, though. There is a story in our local patch with a funeral director, who's not in business any more, who locked the keys in the hearse and had to smash the window to get the coffin out. I judge my funeral director on what sweets they've got in the glovebox. When they give you a lift to the crem or to the graveyard, have a quick look.

COLES You see, we don't do that – because of where I am, because we bury in the village, we walk the coffin ...

BOTTLEY Oh, we do that ...

COLES Yeah, I love doing that, yeah.

BOTTLEY I want that. I want that for mine. I once pressed the button on a crossing and then looked up and realized it was the funeral director.

COLES Well that's it, it's the interesting thing about

FRASER People don't cross themselves as much as they used to, do they?

BOTTLEY I like a hat off. I always get a bit tearful if I see somebody take their hat off.

COLES Coppers salute still; they do round our way, if you can see one.

BOTTLEY Yes, it makes me a bit emotional when I see that.

COLES Some guy did the other day, walked up the hill and a bloke stopped his van, a plumber, got out and stood very respectfully as the cortege went ...

BOTTLEY Oh, though, that backfired. I've taught my children to do that: if a funeral goes past, you have to stand still because that's what I was taught. It was on the high street and the funeral went past, so I got the kids, made them stand still and the funeral director leant out the window and shouted, 'All right, Kate!'

FRASER I buried someone in their back garden the other week . . .

BOTTLEY Perfectly legal.

FRASER Which is extraordinary – I've never done that before . . .

COLES Friend of yours, was it?

FRASER I didn't even know, didn't know it was possible . . .

BOTTLEY It wasn't under a patio or anything, was it, the dead of night?

FRASER No, it was actually this person who was born in this house; they lived in this house all the time, and they phoned up and I didn't even know this was possible. And they phoned up the council and said, 'We'd like him to be buried in the garden, under his apple tree.' And his kids came and dug the hole, and he was buried in his back garden under the apple tree. I mean, they say they're never going to sell the house and so . . .

BOTTLEY You'd have to put it in the deeds, that's all.

COLES Barbara Cartland.

FRASER I thought it was extraordinarily beautiful . . .

COLES She was buried in the back garden.

FRASER Is that right?

COLES Yeah.

BOTTLEY Quite a big back garden though, I would imagine.

COLES It was quite big . . . Our cemetery is up the hill, so I was coming down after a funeral (this was last year), and I was wearing – I like to dress up – big ceremony, so cloak and a biretta and everything. And I was walking down the hill and I was quite pleased with myself having taken the trouble to dress up like that. And a white van went past and a bloke leaned out and he looked at me and he went, 'Oi, f***ing Dumbledore.' [*laughter*]

FRASER Is that what he said?

COLES Dumbledore.

BOTTLEY Have you had selfies at funerals?

COLES Oh yeah, lots now.

BOTTLEY I get that all the time. They sort of sidle up to you and I go, 'How did you know the deceased?' 'He was my grandad.' 'I'm so sorry about your grandad.' 'Can I have a private word with you in the vestry?' 'Yes, of course you can.' So, we go into the vestry and it's, 'Can I have a picture?' [*laughter*] 'Yeah, of course you can.' . . . Selfies . . .

COLES That happens everywhere now, doesn't it?

BOTTLEY Yeah, yeah.

COLES I have one. I was doing a funeral last year . . .

BOTTLEY Don't happen to Giles though, does it, Giles?

FRASER Doesn't.

COLES *Newsnight* audiences aren't really into selfies . . .

BOTTLEY No, they aren't really a selfie sort, are they?

COLES I was doing one last year and it was a crem and I was there and the hearse was arriving and this bloke, a mourner, came up to me, dark suited and very solemnly, and he took my arm and he just went, 'Vicar?' And I said, 'Yes.' He went, 'You're a terrible dancer.'

BOTTLEY He's right.

COLES He was right, yeah.

BOTTLEY Have you done a funeral that you were late for? The one funeral that you ever . . .

COLES Once.

BOTTLEY One. Have you ever been late for one?

FRASER No, I've never been late for one, no.

BOTTLEY I have – one – never do it again.

FRASER I can't, that's too much.

COLES There was a traffic jam on the A14. I was on my way to the crem. I was only five minutes late but it felt terrible.

BOTTLEY And I perfected the art of getting all my robes on at traffic lights, that funeral, and it's never left me, that skill. I can completely robe up in the front of a Ford Ka.

FRASER One of the things I find most moving about funerals is when you do funerals – and this is not something that you can really do at modern memorial services – when you do funerals of someone who's, like – obviously had been a wrong un . . .

BOTTLEY Oh, women stood at a distance with a single red rose, they're my favourite.

FRASER But no, but sometimes there's nobody, so there's really nobody there. So you're the only person that's doing it. And you talk about forgiveness and you know all of the stuff – where the liturgy carries the weight – because at a memorial service, generally speaking, what you do is you say how great the person was. But what do you actually do when the person wasn't great? I once did a funeral of someone who'd clearly been a paedophile. There was nobody else at this funeral. And suddenly the words of the funeral service, about forgiveness and so forth, they come alive in ways that they don't really when you're just sort of eulogizing the person, which is not possible.

BOTTLEY Those ones, you know, those really terrible ones are few and far between. The hardest funerals I find are obviously the ones where the coffin's not big enough, that's tough; women who are forty-four with two kids. I find those really difficult. But the hardest ones I find are where I have nothing to say. So, you go and see the family and you say, tell me about the person, and it's either 'We're glad he's dead' or 'We're glad she's dead', or they've got nothing to tell you and all you've got is crosswords and you've got to spin it out for twenty minutes. 'They like crosswords and *Countdown*', and you think, I've got nothing to say about her.

COLES In a very real sense life is like a crossword . . .

BOTTLEY Like a puzzle of sorts.

COLES Those three little letters G O D make the whole thing come together.

BOTTLEY You're, like, trying desperately to spin something out; those are awful.

FRASER I lost my faith after a funeral and I hadn't been a clergy long enough. I did the funeral of a child, and it was in this huge great big barn of a church in the Black Country. And there was just Mum and her friend and one other woman. And there was this small coffin. And it was so utterly horrible that when it had finished – and Mum had cut herself and it was bleeding, it was so utterly horrible – and I honestly thought this is just all bollocks, all the stuff: there's nothing I can believe about. And I did about – I don't know – about a month, two months, but your job's a vicar so you have to go and you have to celebrate the Eucharist. You have to give the sermons and you have to – because you can't just say next Sunday morning, 'I'm sorry, guys, this isn't really – I'm not going to do this . . .'

BOTTLEY It's not my thing any more.

FRASER Not my thing today. And I tell you what, I've always been extremely pleased when people – the Creed being we believe in God, the Father almighty – I actually felt that they were carrying me during that whole time and it felt like this was the faith of the Church. I'm sort of in this place; but, my word, that darkness can stay with you for a very long time.

COLES But then you know part of our job as disciples is 'My God, my God, why hast thou forsaken me?'

FRASER To carry the darkness.

COLES Yeah, we know that. And sometimes light as well. I remember doing a funeral in my first parish and it was a real lesson. I was called to go and see the son of a woman who'd died, the worst street in the worst part of town. And I got there and there was a kind of smashed-up house, windows kicked in, door kicked in, boarded up. Went in there and there was her son and he had learning difficulties. It was dark, my feet stuck to the floor. They said, 'Would you like a cup of tea?' Really? 'No thank you.' That kind of thing. And I was, to my shame, kind of perfunctory about it; he had nothing particular to say about her. I made some assumptions, I made some notes, I left. Turned up a week later at a crematorium funeral, three hundred and fifty people there.

BOTTLEY Wow.

COLES And I thought it must be for somebody else, but it wasn't, it was for her. And then afterwards I was talking – feeling quite emotional about it already – and there was a guy there, and he was a young guy, mixed heritage, in a British army officer's uniform, and I said to him, 'Are you connected to her?' And it turned out that she had been the woman on that estate who had been the unofficial love and care-giver to all the lost kids, so kids who had chaotic backgrounds, no parents, often in care, ASBO'd out of the town centre, permanently excluded from school – she took them in, she wiped their noses, she put plasters on their knees. She wasn't sentimental, there was nothing kind of fluffy about it at all, but she just loved them.

FRASER That's a privilege, that's a massive privilege . . .

COLES And I remember he said – obviously his own story was fascinating – and he said that if it hadn't been for her he would never have believed that life could be better. She just put in front of him the example of life being better. And I vowed I would never ever again make assumptions about people.

BOTTLEY Very wise.

COLES Based on the things we make assumptions about people.

FRASER I used to have to deal with quite a lot of fights at funerals . . .

COLES Oh yeah . . .

BOTTLEY Oh, first funeral I ever did I split up a fight in the car park. I'm quite proud of that.

FRASER When I was in the Black Country there was lots and lots of times when – the fight usually went like this. It was often the person in the front row was handcuffed to a . . .

BOTTLEY Officer, yeah. I've had those, yeah, yeah.

FRASER . . . to a prison warden. And what would happen is the prison wardens want to go quite quickly, because this is their teatime or they want to go. So, when the coffin's been lowered and I've said the blessing, then that's the point at which the prison guard wants to take the prisoner . . . well, obviously, it's this guy's day out and it's his mum's funeral and so it would all kick off – you f***ing this and you f***ing that – and things would start to fly and you'd be standing there trying to look pious in the middle of it.

BOTTLEY Mine was the classic, the family that they didn't know about, you know, one of those ones . . . Have you had a few of those? So, two brothers – but they didn't know about each other – and we've got a fist fight in the car park; never underestimate the power of a five-foot ginger woman to split two fighting men up. I just went, 'Stop it. Stop it. Now.' Like that, and they just went, 'Ooh', like that and jumped . . .

FRASER In your dog collar?

BOTTLEY Yeah, in my dog collar, full robes: 'Stop it. Stop it. Out.' And they just burst apart, it was amazing. I was like – Oh, come on! – little rush of power.

COLES But everybody dies, don't they?

FRASER Yeah.

BOTTLEY Yeah, yeah.

COLES Great and small, it doesn't really – at the end of it you will come to that same point.

BOTTLEY One of the hardest things, I think, about being a parish priest is when the ones you really loved die. You've got someone in the parish who's really on your side, who's one of your team. And my friend, Jean, was coming to the end of her life and I went to visit her and she was one of those women that was always really worried about how you were. So she would always ask me every service, 'And how are you and how are the kids? You're always looking after everybody else, who's looking after you?' One of those kinds of women. And I went to visit her and she said, 'I'm really worried about my

19

funeral.' I said, 'Why's that?' And she went, 'Well, will you be able to do it?' I said, 'Look, I'm a professional, it's what we do. So, I'll do the visit, I'll be professional, I'll do your funeral, I'll be professional, I'll do the burial, I'll be professional, I'll do the wake, I'll be professional, but then when I get home that'll be my time and I'll get home and I'll put my pyjamas on and I'll hug my kids and I'll go in the fridge and have a bottle of champagne in there and I'll open that and I'll drink it straight down and that's when I'll say goodbye to you.' And she laughed. Anyway, she died and I did the funeral. I did everything I said: I did a really good job, I was really proud of myself and I held it and held it and held it, and those tears were prickling the back of me eyes and a lump in me throat. And I got home and I could feel myself walking up the drive and I just had to get to that door before I could let it go. And as I got to the door of the house, of the vicarage, there was a bottle of champagne . . .

FRASER Oh, that's lovely.

BOTTLEY . . . on the doorstep, and a little note from her that said, 'Today's the day of my funeral, drink this and enjoy it.'

COLES That's so nice.

FRASER I'm going to cry at that.

BOTTLEY It was beautiful, it was a beautiful, beautiful thing.

COLES What about . . .

BOTTLEY And that's the privilege, isn't it?

COLES The other thing you see, of course, is just how incredibly vulnerable old people can be at the end of their lives. I remember doing a funeral once for a guy who'd been a Fleet Street editor, huge life, knew everybody, a character, da, da, da, da, da . . . died in a nursing home. They were expecting a huge funeral – seven people came. Because he'd just kind of outlived his own reputation.

BOTTLEY Well, I had one the other week where no one apparently liked him. He had two hundred there. I thought, well, somebody must have liked . . . His family said no one really liked him.

FRASER I buried my best friend about . . .

BOTTLEY I'm sorry.

FRASER . . . about – I'm going to cry . . .

BOTTLEY You two, what are you like?

FRASER . . . oh God, it's getting me going.

BOTTLEY Your bladder's near your eye.

FRASER Sorry, God, thank you, I did it – I buried him about, I don't know, about four months ago now and it was just the hardest thing ever to do. Those people that you – that you love; they're just impossible to do.

BOTTLEY People that you love. Do you do family?

COLES Well, I did. I had a cousin who I loved and I took her funeral and I said I would never do a family funeral again. And my father died a couple of years ago. Weirdest thing was, the funeral directors are my mates and we work together all the time . . .

BOTTLEY Did they go all professional on you?

COLES Yeah, no bants. There was no bants at all and it was all very sort of quite right too. And you know, I've done hundreds of funerals and I know how it works. My partner David, who's also ordained, took the funeral. The funny thing was I can't remember a thing about it, not a thing.

BOTTLEY Ah, you see, that's it with funerals: you don't remember the lyrics, they won't remember the lyrics, but they will remember the tune. So, they will remember whether you were warm, whether you were friendly, whether you were kind. They won't actually remember what you said; it's the way you carry yourself, the way you hold . . . Sometimes I'll say to the widow, 'He'd be very proud, you carried yourself beautifully.' And they seem to really like that because obviously, because we do a lot of them. You know what you're having, yeah?

COLES Oh yeah.

BOTTLEY Oh, I know what I'm having.

FRASER So, I'll tell you what I want. Let me just tell you. I don't like this business – now we might have a debate . . .

BOTTLEY It's not a celebration of life.

FRASER It is not a celebration . . .

BOTTLEY Don't want a celebration of life.

FRASER I want lots of people all dressed in black.

BOTTLEY Yes.

FRASER I want, either way, I've said this to my wife already, I want lots of beautiful women with, like, things down; no one knows who they are . . .

BOTTLEY Jackie Kennedy, Jackie Kennedy at JFK's, that's what I want. I want the whole veil thing. I've already primed several of my male friends to stand at a distance and weep alone, like they were the other men.

COLES Well, all I want's a *Ring* Cycle. [*laughter*] That's what I'm going to have.

BOTTLEY Don't worry, you'll go before us; we'll make sure you get what you want.

FRASER But proper Mass as well, proper Mass.

BOTTLEY Oh, full on. I mean, I'm not even that High Church and I want the whole – I want the roads cleared; I want the traffic stopped . . .

FRASER Stop all the clocks.

BOTTLEY Weeping, wailing, gnashing of teeth, rending of garments. I don't want anybody to celebrate anything; it's really sad and I'm dead.

COLES Have you had graveside disasters? Anyone fall in?

BOTTLEY Yes. Have you had the dove?

COLES No, I've had a dog.

BOTTLEY Have you had the doves released? So, the dove release: so, we did the funeral, the wife, the kids are stood there with a little cage, and I go, 'What's that?' They go, 'Got a dove to release, Vicar. Don't worry about it.' So, I do the final blessing, the funeral director swoops in and goes, 'Since time immemorial the dove has been a symbol of peace and unity.' And I went, 'Whoa, whoa, blessing's final words, that's the last thing they hear. What's this all about?' He said, 'Oh, we release a dove.

It's the spirit of Carl going up into . . .' I said, 'It's not. But pass it 'ere.' So, I got hold of this dove and we released her. There's 'Ain't it beautiful?' Then sparrow hawk – phumph – straight down and got it. Straight down. It's not Carl now, is it? [*laughter*]

FRASER Coles has just lost it.

BOTTLEY Absolutely true.

FRASER Coles just lost it!

BOTTLEY And they were playing 'The Heart Will Go On' by Celine Dion at the time.

FRASER But there's something interesting about – I know there'll be people out there who think we're superstitious and they'll think religion is superstitious.

BOTTLEY Oh, the folk religion.

FRASER But here's an extraordinary thing. So, one of the things that I was amazed at when I was first a curate is this combination of belief which is don't believe in God, don't believe in all that church stuff, 'cos that's all rubbish. But I believe he's up there looking down on us. And I was thinking, so, people believe in eternal life, as it were, or some version of that, without actually believing in God. And that's quite a common thing, that is.

BOTTLEY Well, it's that whole – when you walk past the graveyard at night and there's a can of Fosters on the gravestone or the mobile phone. It's that folk religion stuff, isn't it? I had to have a debate with a woman not so long ago about why it might not be a good idea to have a glow-in-the-dark Buddha in the churchyard and she couldn't see a problem with that at all. She didn't know what the issue is with glow-in-the-dark Buddhas in there – in a thirteenth-century churchyard.

COLES Strange requests. Do you have the thing about, quite often, about what people want to be buried with, and we're closed for burials but we have cremated remains buried in the churchyard, and of course that's very strictly rule governed and I would never, for example, think for a second of allowing someone to be buried with the ashes of their treasured pets who they've loved all their lives – because I wouldn't do that, Kate.

BOTTLEY Me neither, me neither.

FRASER Okay, have you got anything crossed there? Have you got your fingers crossed?

BOTTLEY I wouldn't do that either.

FRASER I can't see.

BOTTLEY I wouldn't turn my back and walk away from the hole as they're putting things in.

COLES Someone told me the other day, there was a vicar who was saying that someone was dying and she wanted to be buried with the ashes of her dog, and the vicar, who was punctilious, said, 'I'm afraid that's not allowed.' And she said, 'No dog in grave, no me in church.' Never came to church again.

BOTTLEY Wow.

FRASER Oh, is that right?

COLES Yeah.

BOTTLEY I do forget, though, that not everybody's got the connection with death that we've got. So sometimes if we've got ashes on the side in the hallway waiting to be buried or whatever, and the kids bring their friends round for tea and I go, 'Oh, crikey, that's not normal, is it, that you've just got, like, Mrs Jones's ashes on the table in the hallway with a small tealight next to it?' But I love doing funerals.

COLES Me too. And it is the greatest privilege of what we do . . .

FRASER It completely is, it is – completely is. Yeah, and I think we laugh about it sometimes because actually it's really hard. You know, there's times when it's so bloody hard to do it, and especially when you've had some connection with people, but also when you find out their stories and people who've had such tragedy in their lives and you're just there trying to sort of bring all that together. I often have a drink afterwards.

COLES There's the other one – the other one which is – I hadn't seen this coming and it's a big one – is when the person who you're burying has told you something on their deathbed, which you cannot ever share with anyone and has needed to be sorted before they go into death. And that's something that's just with you, and you take it to God and nowhere else. Do you know that one? And sometimes you go back to the vicarage – I remember once going back and someone had told me something and I just walked round my study, no one was at home, and I couldn't sit or settle. I just had to, you know, process.

FRASER Yeah, yeah, that's very familiar, that's very familiar to me, yeah. It can take a couple of days for me afterwards.

COLES Oh well, rest eternal grant unto them, O Lord, and let light perpetual shine upon them. May they rest in peace.

BOTTLEY And rise in glory.

FRASER And rise in glory. [*in unison*]

COLES Amen.

BOTTLEY Amen.

Music: 'Another One Bites the Dust' by Queen

Marriage

Broadcast on Monday 26 August 2019, at 11 a.m.

Presenters: **RICHARD COLES**
                    KATE BOTTLEY
                    GILES FRASER

Producer: **NEIL MORROW**

Series editor: **CHRISTINE MORGAN**

Music: 'Marry You' by Bruno Mars

COLES I'm the Reverend Richard Coles and once again I'm joined by my fellow clergy, the Reverends Giles Fraser and Kate Bottley, and we're gathered here together to muse on weddings. Now, as we've just heard, Bruno Mars is very keen on people saying 'I do'. But I'm wondering, fellow vicars Kate and Giles, are you doing as much of that as you used to do?

BOTTLEY Absolutely not. I think my peak was – I did thirty-six weddings in one year but I haven't done a wedding now for about eighteen months, I think it must be. So my wedding muscle has not been exercised properly – that sounds ruder than I meant, my wedding muscle.

FRASER When I was a curate, I used to do five on a Saturday. They were just piled up.

BOTTLEY Wow.

FRASER And there were so many of them, if you were five minutes late you lost a hymn; if you were ten minutes late you lost two hymns; and if you were fifteen minutes late it didn't happen – didn't happen.

BOTTLEY But you're like this, aren't you, you're really strict about the rules in the churches where you do it, because I'm pretty lax. I'm pretty laid back. But you were telling me that you don't allow people to do videos and filming.

FRASER I don't like videos. I'm agin the video guy.

BOTTLEY But you're an attention-seeking nightmare! Surely you love the video?

COLES But it's not about Giles on the wedding day, is it? [*laughter*] It's not about us, is it?

FRASER No, it's just . . .

BOTTLEY Isn't it?

FRASER I think there's a serious point about modern weddings. They can become much more narcissistic than I remember them being when I started. It's like my special day, all about me . . .

BOTTLEY You grumpy soul.

FRASER But, you know, the Posh and Becks sitting in their thrones and all that sort of stuff. And I suspect that – well, I don't know – I have got no empirical evidence of this but I feel that the sort of grander the wedding the less successful the marriage. I wonder if that's true. There you go, look at Bottley's face – it's just gone . . .

BOTTLEY I can't believe your sort of grumpy soul and stuff. I love it. So, one of the best weddings I ever did was where they had matching Labrador puppies to walk down the aisle with. It was just amazing. And their leads matched the bridesmaids' dresses. I love all that. I match my shoes and my nails to the theme of the wedding. I love it. It's great.

COLES It can go too far in that direction. I used to be in a very weddingy church, when I started out, but there was one very nice couple I did and we had the wedding rehearsal the night before and it had all gone very swimmingly, and they'd been to wedding preparation, been very attentive, and then just as they were going the bloke said to me, 'There is one thing.' I said, 'What's that?' He said, 'We're actually doing a pirate theme, so we wondered would you mind dressing up as Long John Silver?' [*laughter*]

FRASER Seriously?

BOTTLEY And you said 'darling'.

COLES No, I didn't. I was rather frosty, actually.

BOTTLEY Were you?

COLES Yeah. I said, 'No, I'm not going to dress up as Long John Silver.' Couldn't get a parrot: how could I source a parrot overnight?

FRASER This wasn't a wedding that I conducted but it was one that I heard about and this speaks to the whole idea of narcissism. All the guests were asked to wear white, so you have to go out and buy white shoes – I don't have a pair of white shoes – but white shoes, white suit and all of the congregation was in white. And then 'Here Comes the Bride' starts and the bride comes down in scarlet! And it's just – oh, my word, could it be any clearer: me, me, me?

BOTTLEY They'd look so good on the photos . . .

COLES Do you preach at a wedding?

FRASER Yes, always, yeah.

BOTTLEY I'd always do a talk. I always talk about love and where I think love comes from and all that sort of stuff. Do you?

COLES Yeah, I always do, but sometimes I still make a joke about Jedward and I've noticed that nobody gets that any more. [*laughter*]

BOTTLEY Time to retire that joke. Do you do the same talk?

FRASER No, but there's a structure to it. But I never write them down. I've never got any of my sermons written down, so I always just speak.

BOTTLEY You mean making it up off the top of your head, Giles, because you haven't prepared properly?

FRASER No, no, I always – I mean I only ever preach extemporary, I only ever – or I've only ever preached extemporary, so that's just like . . . It's a different sort of preparation.

COLES Have you ever had a 'no show', or have you ever had to stop a wedding?

BOTTLEY No, I've never had to stop a wedding. I've had the groom forget the rings and had to go, so I had to slooow the wedding down. I've never had a 'no show'. But I always do – at the rehearsal – say, 'If there's anything you need to tell me, you need to tell me now.' I always do that. But no, I've never had a 'no show'.

FRASER I've never had a 'no show' either.

BOTTLEY I think that's just on telly, that's just on *Friends*, isn't it?

COLES I've had a few . . .

BOTTLEY Have you?

COLES Yeah, I've had a few 'no shows'.

BOTTLEY Oh, come on, let me get comfy, tell us . . . [*laughter*]

COLES It was in my first parish, where we were a sort of a wedding factory and – I say 'a few' – I must have had three or four 'no shows'.

FRASER Wow.

COLES Yeah, just no one came.

BOTTLEY How do you manage that, then? How do you –
I don't mean how do you manage that, I mean how do
you manage that? What do you do, what do you say?

COLES Ladies and gentlemen, I'm very sorry, I'm afraid the
bride and groom haven't made it.

FRASER Wow.

COLES Yeah. I've had someone say – any reason why they
can't get married? – and I've had to stop.

BOTTLEY Have you?

COLES Yeah, once.

BOTTLEY But mate, you are the film set . . . I didn't know
that was real!

COLES No, I know . . . Have you ever had it?

FRASER No, never.

COLES Oh, and in the end it wasn't because it was a legal
reason why. It was just that this person thought that the
bride should be marrying him not her. But we had to
stop and calm him down.

FRASER Oh, wow!

BOTTLEY Oh, the arrogance.

FRASER What an arse. So . . .

COLES I think he might have been right. [*laughter*]

BOTTLEY Awkward.

FRASER Yeah, that's a bit late, isn't it? I always tell people at
wedding rehearsals, to the best man and to the groom, to
check the bottom of their shoes. Do you do this . . .

BOTTLEY Oh, I do that, I do that, yeah.

FRASER ... because it's a very common thing to write on the bottom of your shoes, something like 'help me', or something like that, because when you kneel down and you're at the front of the church and everybody in the congregation can therefore see the bottom of your shoes and someone's written – some wag has written 'help me' on the bottom of the shoes, or worse. I've had worse than that.

BOTTLEY I have a tool belt at my weddings, which has got a sewing kit in it. It's got black socks, it's got spare buttons, all those sorts of things, so that everything's done. But...

FRASER You're kidding me?

BOTTLEY No, I'm not kidding you. Of course I'm not kidding you. I have it all ready for them just in case. I even have a spare pair of women's shoes, just in case. And they have been used. You see there was an occasion when one mother of the bride turned up and she got her heel stuck in the grate as she came into church, broke the heel off, so she had my shoes and the only other shoes I could find, at the time, were the wellies that I keep in the back of the car for when I walk the dog. So, I had to marry them in dog-walking wellies.

COLES That's nice. There's an interesting one, though, Kate.

BOTTLEY Go on.

COLES ... because you're a lady vicar ...

BOTTLEY A lady vicar – vicarette – which makes me sound like a nicotine patch.

COLES . . . but I wonder if that changes weddings because you'll kind of understand perhaps a bit more about boob and breast management and stuff, that gentleman vicars probably don't?

BOTTLEY Well, I had a groom and said to the groom, 'Is there a reason that you've got white sports socks on with your black shoes and your black suit?' And he said, 'Well, it won't matter, she won't notice.' And I said, 'She will notice.' 'She won't notice.' 'She will notice. So, what colour socks has the best man got on, your Kevin?' And Kevin had got black socks on. So, I made the best man and the groom swap socks.

FRASER Urghh. That's not nice.

BOTTLEY So that the groom had black socks on. And . . .

COLES And you say *he's* grumpy.

BOTTLEY And I got the payback because when the bride got to the top of the aisle and he turned round to her and said, 'You look beautiful,' she went, '*You* do, but why's your Kevin wearing white socks?'

FRASER Do you do wedding preparation?

BOTTLEY Errm, sometimes. [*laughter*]

FRASER Because I always think about it as . . .

BOTTLEY Are you my bishop? Yes I do. Are you not . . . sort of . . .

FRASER Oh, I see, I see, I see. Because that whole idea of – I mean, I think this used to be the case – I've never done it like this – you just have this idea of a married couple coming to what might be a celibate man, who's drawing stick drawings of people. And this is the sort of historical joke, isn't it, about wedding preparations . . .

BOTTLEY It used to be the condom talk, didn't it, in the vicarage; we had that. As a good, young, Evangelical couple in our early twenties we had to go to the vicarage to have the condom talk.

FRASER I'm afraid I don't know what the condom talk is.

BOTTLEY Ah, you sit down with the vicar in the front room and he pours you weak tea and then he talks about contraception, and it's all very, very awkward. It's sounding more awkward.

COLES I just can't imagine doing that.

BOTTLEY Can't you?

COLES The most awkward moment I had in wedding preparation was signing the chit to get the groom out of his community service! But I've never had a condom conversation.

BOTTLEY Yeah, and it's that – it's always that awkward moment when you're saying, 'How did you meet?' And, of course, these days they're still a bit shifty about that – having met online. And, like, everyone meets like that now. They say, 'We met on Plenty of Fish.' You're, like – yeah, that's how people meet.

FRASER What is it called?

BOTTLEY Plenty of Fish? Or Tinder. Do you not know these things? Oh, Grandad!

FRASER [*laughter*]

COLES I thought it was a pescatarian delivery service. [*laughter*]

FRASER Plenty of Fish.

BOTTLEY Have you never swiped right?

COLES No, I haven't. I've never done that.

BOTTLEY I never have, obviously, I am happily married, but, yeah, when they talk about – oh, I swiped right on him . . .

COLES But what I do find, and this is something I learnt when I was at Knightsbridge, because lots of people wanted to get married in Knightsbridge because it was a posh church. Because of the law, to qualify to do so they had to come for six months and that was the best pastoral tool we ever had, was getting young couples to come to church for six months. And we were very strict about it. But all of our growth that came about, in sort of the under-forties, came about as a result of that because they just begin to get involved in the life of the church. And the best wedding prep you can do is say, 'Come to church and see what we do.'

FRASER Exactly right.

BOTTLEY And actually what happens is – June, who serves the teas and coffees, comes and sidles up to them, asks them about their big day, gets really excited about it and then they come back to the carol service the following year and then eventually they come back for a christening and before they know it they're part of the church family and they can't think about not coming.

FRASER And it's when June takes Saturday off to go to the wedding . . .

BOTTLEY Yeah, to go to the wedding, sits at the back.

FRASER And then actually – they're a part of it. Why is it that we don't so much like weddings?

COLES Well, I – speaking personally – I think with a funeral that's very much to do with what we're all about and most people still find they connect to that somehow. I think we've sort of lost weddings. I'm not sure we ever should have really had weddings. In the old days, when weddings were, kind of, civil ceremonies that were then vaguely blessed at the church door, that's probably about right. But we kind of brought them into church; we turned them into a whole big thing. But we'll never win that battle against people who, for whatever reason, are just having their special day. So, I think, in a way, we don't feel particularly connected to it, do you think?

FRASER No, that might be right. I mean I also think that there's an actual practical difference – in that a wedding is usually organized, like, a year and a half in advance, and so someone calls you up, terribly nervous, and they say, 'Do you know what colour the flowers are going to be?' or some sort of organizational matter about next September, of which I really don't – I don't care at this stage . . .

COLES Not really high on your agenda, is it, Giles? No.

FRASER So, it becomes this sort of long-drawn-out thing. Whereas, if you die your funeral actually happens reasonably soon and you don't have all of that extraordinary faff about funerals.

BOTTLEY The best thing, though, is when you do a series of services for a family. So, when you add those moments of connection and you see the story coming through, that's actually what I really love, is that when you know that the kid who's the bridesmaid you christened three years ago, and then you look over at Granny and think, I'll be burying you next month. And you know that sort of . . .

COLES Thanks!

BOTTLEY That's what I like, is when actually you're involved in those stories.

COLES I like wedding rehearsals. It's funny, when I was in a band, I liked the sound check more than the gig. There's something about the practice more than the real thing I quite like. And my favourite ever wedding story – it was a wedding rehearsal and it was when I was at the posh church in London and it was quite an elaborate ceremony, it being a posh church, and he was a military guy, so there were all sorts of guards of honour and swords. You know in the bit where they say, 'If anyone knows any reason why these persons may not be joined in . . .', well if you're in the military all the officers half draw their swords . . .

BOTTLEY Just in case?

COLES There's this kind of flash of cutlery at that moment. It's very exciting. But anyway – he was a military man and obviously used to drill, and when it came to the wedding rehearsal I said – all right, da, da, da – and I said, 'Then he'll come up for the blessing, come up to the high altar, kneel, I'll bless you and then we'll go off to the vestry and we'll sign the registers' – as indeed you do. So, that all went fine. They come up for a blessing. I blessed them and I went to walk into the vestry and, you know that thing where you think something's wrong . . .

BOTTLEY Something's happened, yeah.

COLES . . . they were following me but they were still on their knees. They literally . . .

BOTTLEY Because you hadn't told them to stand up?

COLES . . . because I hadn't told them to stand up. So, there she was in this huge dress and him in his uniform literally on their knees . . .

FRASER I'm absolutely gobsmacked.

BOTTLEY That's a great one.

COLES I know, I mean it was sort of mad. But then cognitive dissonance, I don't know, military discipline – if you don't tell them exactly what to do they won't do it.

BOTTLEY My favourite one was the groom who thought it would be a really good idea to have the wedding rings in a small novelty safe and he brought that to the rehearsal. And of course, being the vicar that likes to say yes, I said, 'Yes of course you can have them in a small novelty safe.

Just make sure you know how to get the safe open.' So, at the rehearsal all worked fine, the safe . . .

FRASER Oh, no.

BOTTLEY . . . of course, it didn't on the day. We had to get out – fortunately I had my tool belt, Giles, with a spanner in it, so I popped that sucker open. See – always be prepared!

FRASER Do you – because you're a pleaser and you like to say yes to people – do you let them say 'obey'?

BOTTLEY No. I won't say obey or have that reading.

COLES That's an interesting one. I always think . . .

BOTTLEY No, of course they can. They can have what they want but I would counsel against it.

COLES But you manage that?

BOTTLEY Yeah, I'd manage it. I'd talk about it in the talk.

COLES Well, I had the thing where they said, 'We want traditional language.' I then read them the 1662 . . . the kind which uses the word 'fornication' . . .

FRASER . . . they have no understanding.

BOTTLEY I've had that at funerals where people have gone, 'Oh we want the traditional language.' And I say, 'You don't, you really don't want that.'

FRASER People actually want reproduction furniture, so they actually want the copy of the traditional service with thees and thous but without . . .

COLES So, you can use the 1928 version (of course with the permission of your bishop). There are ways of getting round that.

FRASER We have to talk about the reception because the reception can be a nightmare. Do you always get put on the grannies' table?

BOTTLEY Yes, I always get invited to the reception. Early on in my vicar life I would always say yes, because I thought that's what you were supposed to do because then they might come back and have a christening, and do all that sort of stuff . . .

FRASER You don't go, Richard?

COLES I'm of an age now where my friends have got children of marriageable age, so I'm quite often asked if I would go and marry them, and then of course as a family friend I go to the reception. But normally, no, I don't. I actually haven't got time.

BOTTLEY Yeah. What I've started doing now is I say, 'You don't want to waste forty quid on my dinner; I'll just come for a drink,' and that's what I do.

COLES Rabbis do that. Rabbis go for a drink but don't stay for dinner, and I think we could take a tip from rabbis on that one. I just don't have time – and also, it's a Saturday and you've got Sunday the next day . . . Of course, Giles, you'd always be prepared midweek for your Sunday services, have the sermon written. But for others – and you too, Kate – for others like me, I need that Saturday night to get ready.

BOTTLEY But when I do pitch up, I do get put on the grannies' table. And you spend the whole reception going, 'YES, LOVELY SERVICE,' and no one has anything to say to you apart from, 'Lovely service, Vicar.' And then I have to go, 'Would you like me to cut that up for you?' And that's basically the way that the whole reception goes.

COLES And don't you think also . . .

BOTTLEY It's a bit like having lunch with *you* really. [*laughter*]

COLES I love it when you cut my food up.

BOTTLEY If I do go, I'll be the first on the dance floor.

COLES It's normally the bride and groom – you know that, don't you?

BOTTLEY Well, after the bride and groom. I'll go in . . .

FRASER You became famous really, didn't you, for that wedding video that you did. So, what was the . . .

COLES Flash mob Kate.

FRASER Flash . . .

BOTTLEY That flash mob vicar.

FRASER Remind me what happened, then.

BOTTLEY I was the curse of the clergy all over the country for about six months after that because all the brides and grooms asked, 'Can we have a dance at our wedding?' I did Gary and Tracy's wedding, and Gary and Tracy wanted something different and I suggested a flash mob. So I started dancing, they started dancing, the whole . . .

FRASER What was it to?

BOTTLEY It was 'Everybody Dance' . . . which makes me twitch now, like that. It got ten million hits on YouTube.

COLES It's brilliant.

BOTTLEY Thank you.

COLES There's a lovely bit where one of the old ladies walks . . . [*giggles*] and I'm sure she was . . .

BOTTLEY She was just going to the loo. Auntie Betty's got a bladder the size of a walnut, that's what it was.

COLES But it was really good and it did make me think this is a vicar who enjoys a wedding, and you don't often see that.

BOTTLEY Well, it was about saying yes. I mean, for me, what has happened so much for the church is that people come to us expecting us to say – No, you can't have a video; no, you can't have this; no, you can't have that. And I just thought it would be nice to say yes to a few things. Got me into all sorts of trouble but I . . .

FRASER Did it get you into trouble?

BOTTLEY Oh yeah, got me into all sorts of bother.

FRASER Who got you into – the bishop?

BOTTLEY No, no – the bishop was fine but lots of people were very angry about me dancing in church . . .

COLES Celebrating in church!

BOTTLEY I know! I like to remind them that King David danced in the Bible and he did it with no pants on. So at least I didn't take it that far. Or did I?

FRASER The problem with this conversation is that we're in danger of actually missing another side of weddings entirely, which is – and they're not so funny – but they are the really beautiful weddings where you have two people that are just looking at each other and you think – oh my word, that's just fantastic. And I mean that's – I have to say – it's an enormous privilege to be a part of that. I mean there is the comedy side, there is all of that side, but there is that absolute joy to be a part of it.

BOTTLEY And it's when it catches you by surprise. So, I've done it before now where I'll admit I've been a bit of a snob and I've gone – oh, they're a bit rough – or – I don't like that frock she's wearing – or – that dress shows off her tattoos. And then you get there and you go – and it's like God going – oi, catch yourself on – you know and you stand there and you go – oh, this is just the most beautiful thing. And then you make the mistake of actually looking at the words that you're reading and you can just feel yourself – you feel yourself starting to cry . . .

FRASER I cry, I cry, I def cry. Do you cry?

COLES I cry. I did a wedding and it was a guy who came from Iran and his English fiancée – it was a big wedding – and then her side of the church was absolutely jammed and there were, like, four people on his side of the church, and it turned out that lots of his family had been killed in the revolution and that he had been taken prisoner and had very nearly died and had just got out of the country. I could still feel myself . . .

FRASER Oh my word.

COLES . . . and he cried, and normally it's kind of . . . but then, of course, he cried and everybody cried. I still cry thinking about it now.

BOTTLEY Grooms are the worst criers, though.

COLES Yeah.

BOTTLEY The men always cry more than the women at weddings. So [*laughter*] it's absolutely true. I had a groom and it took him – so, you know when you do the vows and you go, 'I, Brian, take you, Barbara' – or whatever – and it took him twenty minutes to say his own name and her name because he kept going, 'I'm Brian [*shaking*] . . .' I was going, 'It's all right, just breathe.' And at the beginning I was, like, 'Just breathe, just breathe' and he was going – [*intake of breaths*] 'But she just looks so beautiful.' I went, 'Yes I know.' And I was really patient with him for the first ten minutes and then I was, like, going, 'Right, you've got to do this now. Time is money; we've got a reception to get to.' But everyone cheered when he got through his . . .

FRASER I've once got the names wrong.

COLES [*sharp intake of breath*] Oh no, really?

BOTTLEY Oh, Giles.

FRASER Or, a name wrong. I once got a name wrong.

COLES All the way through because they didn't say anything?

FRASER No, no, they did. I got it wrong once and it was a close name to the name. I think we always write the names in big somewhere . . . anyway, I just hadn't looked up. And about three years later I was having a curry in Birmingham and these two people came over and said, 'You're the vicar who got our names wrong at the wedding.'

BOTTLEY They will remember it for ever. Post-it note on their forehead . . . that's what you want to do.

FRASER I know, it's terrible. I know, I know, I know.

BOTTLEY That's what you want to do: Post-it note on their forehead.

COLES I once very nearly accidently married the best man instead of the man. They were from South America and they were from some South American country's navy – I can't remember, the Argentinian navy or something – and it was a big wedding in London and everything. And the father walked her up the aisle with his aide-de-camp as well, so there was a kind of platoon coming up that way. And then they were all bristling with swords and stuff, and I kind of got them mixed up and I very nearly married her to the best man instead of the groom.

FRASER One of the things that gets me about weddings is their wildly inappropriate hymn choices . . .

BOTTLEY 'Fight the good fight'?

FRASER 'Though I walk through the valley of the shadow of death I'll fear no evil.' You think, do you really want to be saying that at your . . .

COLES Yeah. Or 'Dear Lord and Father of mankind, forgive our foolish ways' . . .

BOTTLEY Forgive our foolish ways.

COLES I've got one tomorrow with that.

FRASER Really?

COLES Yeah.

FRASER Do you ever say anything?

COLES I make a joke about it sometimes.

BOTTLEY Talk about wrong music: my friend runs a wedding venue; he was very proud of his first wedding that he did. And this bride had got a CD, *Songs from the Movies*, and she wanted to walk out to Celine Dion, 'My Heart Will Go On'. And he'd got it all sorted, and he pressed the button and it was the theme tune to *Jaws*. [*laughter*] It went – Nah-nah, Nah-nah . . .

COLES Everything can go wrong, even on the most solemn and serious day of your life. My guiding principle is, it's got to be a good experience. These are often a church full of people who never go to church, who have no experience of it at all. The last thing they need is to have some grumpy git making them feel uncomfortable and awkward. So, I always do my very best to make sure they have . . .

BOTTLEY A lovely, lovely time.

COLES But then, you're not a pleaser, Giles.

FRASER I'm really grumpy about people being very, very late, sort of forty minutes late, an hour late. And I'll say to people at rehearsal – please! They say, 'Yes, we'll be on time.' Please be on time. 'Yes, we'll be on time.' And then half an hour after we're supposed to have started, when there are still people sitting in there, I get a text message saying, 'Just finishing off the makeup.' And I'm, like . . . It's hard not to be grumpy, it is hard not to be grumpy.

COLES There was a friend of mine, she was a curate in Lincoln Diocese, and her boss used to just go after twenty minutes. So if they weren't there after twenty minutes he would just go and there would be no wedding, which is very grumpy.

BOTTLEY That is very grumpy.

FRASER That's very, very grumpy.

BOTTLEY You wouldn't be that grumpy, would you?

FRASER No, no, no. I wouldn't be that grumpy. I mean, I've been grumpy ... but I wouldn't go. Well, that's the whole point about having five weddings – if you have five on a Saturday, if you're fifteen minutes late then actually what you're doing is you're affecting the people that come after you. I've stopped a hymn and I've stopped two hymns because they were twelve or so minutes late, so we haven't had the hymns, but I've never done the 'We're not doing it'.

COLES But gone are the days when we would have five weddings queued up, I think, unless of course we were doing illegal weddings.

BOTTLEY Let's be glad they're still getting married in church.

FRASER Yes, yes, yes.

COLES I've had one – a couple of weddings – where I thought I'm not entirely convinced that this couple have ever met before; well, not quite that but where I have thought, actually, I'm not sure this is kosher.

FRASER I tell you what I'm really grumpy about. I'm really grumpy about the Home Office getting involved in weddings these days. So, I have people who get married who I know, part of my congregation, who I know very, very well, but because one of them might be from Africa and might have a Nigerian passport, or something like that, the Home Office are all over this and the idea that we have to sort of go down to the Register Office, which has now become an arm of the Home Office, to seek their permission to do what, in my view, is a religious ceremony . . . that I really am grumpy about. So, that's shocking, that is shocking.

COLES But that's really interesting. I mean, that is a wedding absolutely of our time, isn't it, where people ask those sorts of questions and want to tick all those boxes. There's a difference, isn't there, between the kind of tradition . . . I mean, you've seen my church – it's the perfect church to get married in, gingerbread stone . . .

BOTTLEY Well, I think you'll find it probably isn't. I think you'll find my church is the perfect church – no.

COLES Well, it would be if you were ever in it, Kate. [*laughter*] Mea culpa – yeah, look who's talking. But it is – the thing I notice now, it always used to be bridesmaids would follow the bride and yet now more and more often it's bridesmaids before . . .

BOTTLEY Bridesmaids in first.

COLES . . . so, the bride comes in and makes her grand entrance at the end. Do you stop that?

BOTTLEY No, of course I don't. I say yes.

COLES But what do you think?

BOTTLEY I prefer bridesmaids in second. But I don't lead them in either.

COLES Don't you?

BOTTLEY I walk in, then I turn and nod, and then the bride walks in because everyone wants to see her; they're not actually looking at me.

COLES You should see my cope; they want to see my cope.

BOTTLEY You're working it, girlfriend.

COLES No, but you know, a bride did say that to me once. It was at the posh church where we had some magnificent vestments by Bodley, that are normally in the V&A, and I remember we had this magnificent cope and I put that on, the bride just went – 'No!'

BOTTLEY No, you're upstaging me.

FRASER That wasn't in Boston, was it? That was in Lincolnshire.

COLES No, that was in Knightsbridge.

BOTTLEY You've done crazy weddings, though, with budgets for flowers, where the budget for flowers was like a deficit of a small country.

COLES Well, there were several extravagant ones. I remember a bride's dress that cost eighty thousand quid . . .

FRASER [*sharp intake of breath*]

COLES And it cost fifteen thousand quid to dry clean. And that was a wedding where they spent fifty thousand quid on flowers.

FRASER I've got my mouth just, like, hanging open.

COLES Another one we did, I remember, and it was a very nice guy who works in the City, had lots of money. He came not from a posh background at all but it was a very grand wedding and he was lovely and his wife was too. And they had the reception at the V&A and I said, 'Oh, at the canteen at the V&A?' And they went, 'No, the V&A.' The whole of the V&A. And I remember going along to the reception. They had a band on, and I thought, this is the best Snow Patrol tribute band I've ever seen, and then I thought, *it is* actually Snow Patrol. [*laughter*]

BOTTLEY Yes, but I had Spandau Ballet once at a wedding reception – that was fun.

COLES Real Spandau Ballet?

BOTTLEY Yeah, real Spandau Ballet. They were great.

COLES Oh, that's cool, yeah.

BOTTLEY They were great, really good.

COLES That's the thing about . . .

FRASER Done karaoke once . . .

COLES But I think some of the loveliest weddings I've done have been ones which have been almost not quite clandestine. And of course, most of the weddings I'd most like to do but I'm not able to do are because they're same-sex couples.

FRASER Have you done any sort of quasi – you see, basically, we're not allowed to say this, are we, but we try and go up to the wire as much as we can with same sex. So, we can't call them blessings – the Church blesses bloody battleships but it won't bless two people who love each other. So, we're all grumpy about that, I imagine. But there are ways of going up to the wire about this and nearly doing a wedding, something that almost looks like a wedding, but we're not allowed to say that.

COLES I'm going to plead the fifth on that. [*laughter*]

BOTTLEY And me also.

FRASER I have. I would say I have.

BOTTLEY Yeah, but you're not bothered about getting into trouble like we are.

FRASER Ah, well, you know.

COLES We've talked a lot about the kind of comedy of it, the tragi-comedy of it, the bits and bobs, things that go right, things that go wrong, but what about the spirituality of it?

BOTTLEY Oh, there's always a moment, there's always a moment that even the most cynical of grooms, who's gone, 'I'm only getting married in church because she wanted to.' You know those kinds of things. Which in logic tends to be, but there's always a moment when God gets them, always; you can just see it.

COLES I think it's that thing when all of a sudden everyone realizes that they're doing something that's bigger than them and that, you know, people have been before them and have stood in that place maybe seven hundred years and will hopefully for another seven hundred years be doing that, and they become part of this bigger story, and it's a wonderful story about hope and transformation, you know.

FRASER I completely know. And the idea that you're somehow bringing all that together, that's a joyous thing to do. It's a joyous thing to do. We're very privileged. Well, I am, anyway.

BOTTLEY The best wedding I ever did was for a couple who had learning disabilities and their parents came to see me and said they really wanted to get married: 'Is that possible?' I said, 'Yeah, absolutely, of course it is. I'd be delighted.' But they didn't want a big fuss. And what this kind of misconception is, is that if you get married in church you have to have a white dress, you have to have flowers, you have to have an organ, you have to have loads . . . You don't have to have any of that. I just need two witnesses, a ring and two people who've had their banns read; that's all I need. And they arrived at church in their jeans and their jumpers and we sat in a little circle. We didn't have any music, we didn't have any flowers, we didn't have any of that. They went to the pub for lunch and I blubbed like a baby, all the way through it. And it was the most beautiful wedding I have ever been to in my whole life, including my own.

COLES Oh, that's lovely. A parish priesty thing. I notice now that I'm burying people who got demobbed and got married, and there's lots of pictures they bring of getting married in church. It's not a big do, nobody had any money.

FRASER The fact that I love what you've just said, that's probably where my grumpiness grows out of. That, actually, there is a way of doing this which is not about the sort of celebrity obsessed 'going to be covered by *Hello!* magazine'. There's a way of doing this that actually is utterly beautiful and wonderful, and actually all of that sort of *Hello!* stuff really distracts from it sometimes.

BOTTLEY But I think our job, as clergy, is to search through the distraction and to cut through all that stuff and to find what it's actually really about. And sometimes the layers are lots and that might make us grumpy but actually the reason that we are in that place, and the reason those two people are there, is because they love each other and want to commit for the rest of their lives. And I'm totally on board with that. No matter how much they've spent on flowers.

FRASER Of course. Okay.

COLES Well, what a little ramble we've done, up and down the various aisles over which we've had spurious authority in our years of ministry.

BOTTLEY Ooh, you have got a lovely turn of words, our Richard.

COLES I've had two cappuccinos. We'd just – I'm sure we'd all like to take this opportunity to wish every blessing and every happiness to every bride and groom or groom and groom and bride and bride, however you want to configure it, and may they have much joy with each other.

FRASER Absolutely.
BOTTLEY And also with you.

Music: 'White Wedding' by Billy Idol

Birth

Broadcast on Monday 2 September, at 11 a.m.

Presenters: **RICHARD COLES**
                       KATE BOTTLEY
                       GILES FRASER

Producer: **NEIL MORROW**

Series editor: **CHRISTINE MORGAN**

Music: 'Isn't She Lovely' by Stevie Wonder

COLES Welcome to the final episode in this series of *The Three Vicars*, where three vicars do exactly what it says on the tin. I'm joined, once again, by my fellow Church of England soulmates: the Reverend Kate Bottley and the Reverend Giles Fraser. But in an illogical twist we're finishing at the beginning, that point where children come into our world.

Hatching, matching, dispatching. We've done some matching and dispatching, but hatching, that other – I find I'm doing more and more of it because as the sort of matching dwindles, because we've priced ourselves out of that market, I find we're getting more and more people are coming for baptism, because it's cheaper, and turning that into their big do.

FRASER No!

BOTTLEY Yeah, because people aren't always married, so this is the first, kind of, opportunity that they've got to, sort of, cement their family and say, 'This is us; we're setting our stall out as a unit.' So, I'm finding a lot of people come for baptism or christening, as they call it, without necessarily having done the other bits.

COLES No, and because we don't charge for it that makes it affordable. If you're a parish like mine, which is poor, that makes a big difference to people. So, they come and they get dressed up and it turns into a whole big do. But it means that you have that thing that we enjoy so much, of having a church full of people who are completely unacquainted with our ways. That's fun.

I remember one of the first baptisms I ever did, and it was a baby who was being baptized, but one of the godparents hadn't been baptized, so she wanted to get baptized first, obviously. And she was lovely, but she was unused to church ways and hadn't been fully prepared for this momentous threshold experience. And as she approached the font, she took out her chewing gum and put it on the side of the font.

BOTTLEY Love it.

COLES And then I baptized her and then she put it back in when I'd done. But, I mean, that was respectful.

BOTTLEY But I've had respectful as well. I had a godfather who was in Australia, and we did that whole sort of slight dilemma about can you be a godparent and not actually be in the room? And then I remembered all the stories of the royal family who have godparents by proxy, don't they. So, I thought, it'll be fine, there's a precedent. So, the godfather was in Australia and we got him on Skype on the sort of iPad kind of thing and we cut to him. I'd sent him the order of service and he'd printed it all out – and he'd put his suit on. It was, like, one o'clock in the morning and he'd put his suit on and he stood up for all the hymns and he sat down and everything; he joined in with the whole thing, it was perfect.

FRASER They're my favourite – baptisms. Baptism is my favourite of all of the big things that we do. It's just everybody gathered around the font. This whole idea of this is the serious sort of churchy business.

BOTTLEY But I'm presuming you can see into the font, whereas I can't: the font's too tall for me.

FRASER Don't you have a little step? Or you can do full total immersion. I've done it in the river, in America, where you go and you get the young child. And I learnt something about baptism when I did immersion and the priest said to me, 'Hold the child under . . .' – he was about twelve or something – 'Hold the child under much longer than you think it should be under.'

COLES Good advice.

FRASER And I said, 'Why?' He said, 'Because this is not a washing, this is a drowning.' And actually, the theology is it is much more like drowning. So, Romans talks about you're baptized into the death and resurrection of Jesus. Now, if you tell people who come for their little Johnny being done, this is simulated drowning . . .

BOTTLEY This is death.

FRASER . . . they don't really like it. But that's much more the theology of it. It's a drowning. And you see that, when you do full immersion and they come up and they go [*big intake of breath*] because they've actually – and you get this idea that, oh my word, this is a new life, which is much more theologically interesting than just splashing a little bit of – as if they need washing or something.

BOTTLEY I've done one full immersion and I learnt the lesson that if you blow really hard on a baby's face they go [*sharp intake of breath*], which means that you can dunk them without them breathing in the water. So, if you ever have to do a baby, don't have garlic the night before; quick waft on the baby's face and then all the way under.

FRASER Babies can go under water anyway.

BOTTLEY Yeah, but I'm not risking it. It's not my baby.

COLES Listeners at home, please don't try this without a . . . [*laughter*] without a paediatrician supervising. Have you done an Orthodox or been to an Orthodox baptism . . .

FRASER No.

COLES . . . when the priest – is it *exoflates*? – breathes like the wrath of God across the waters? And the baby is covered in oil and, as slippery as a fish, is dipped in total immersion into the font. And everyone turns up, then you have a big do afterwards.

BOTTLEY Sounds great.

COLES But, then again, no skimping on the sacramentals. They're unlike us with a little kind of . . .

BOTTLEY But do you have splash zone at your baptism?

FRASER I chuck everybody . . .

BOTTLEY Do you chuck it about? I chuck it about a bit. Everybody gets wet, so it's like going to Sea Parks or Sea World or whatever. I mean, there's, like, a zone, where if you sit you're going to get wet. But, of course, the people that haven't been to my christenings before don't know this, so they all snuggle up nice and tight, so they can see what's happening and people who have been before, you can see them just taking about five steps back, leaning back so they don't get wet.

COLES I take a branch from the yews outside, which are the oldest – they're pre-Conquest – and I use a branch of yew. I hope I haven't offended against the laws of yew conservation, but anyway that's what I do. And I sprinkle. And also, we use the water from the font to sprinkle the coffin at a funeral as well. Do you do that?

BOTTLEY Yeah, I do that, yeah. I'm quite Catholic really, you know. I know you think I'm an Evangelical nightmare, but I'm quite a bit of a Catholic.

COLES So, tambourine in one hand and holy water in the other one. That's you, that's the Church of England.

BOTTLEY That's right, crossing myself, one hand in the air, that's the way it works.

FRASER But in terms of birth itself, you're the only one of the three of us that has given birth . . .

BOTTLEY Yeah.

FRASER Does that have a sort of – does it have a sacramental element?

BOTTLEY It's just horrible. [*laughter*] Don't let anyone kid you, it's bloody awful. I know people talk about it being a deep spiritual experience but I just wanted to get it over with as quickly as possible.

FRASER It's a spiritual experience to watch.

BOTTLEY No, it's horrid.

FRASER It is to watch. I mean I haven't done it but I've watched it five times and it's like, yeah, yeah, yeah.

BOTTLEY I've watched it too. I mean, I didn't want to be present at my own births, let alone anybody else's –

giving birth. But I ended up being present at two births, actually of the same woman giving birth, who's . . .

COLES Were you birth partner?

BOTTLEY Yes, I was a birth partner because I buried one of her children. One of her babies died, and then she subsequently had two more children and asked me to be her birth partner at those. So, it was that. And her line was, 'You saw one of my children out of this world, I'd like you to see the rest in.'

FRASER Oh, Kate.

COLES It's sweet. There's times when you're called to post-natal intensive care. I remember baptizing one of my parishioners' sons who was born very, very, very premature – twenty-six weeks, I think it was – and a tiny, tiny, tiny little scrap of life, and he was in the incubator. And having to baptize this tiny, tiny, tiny little human, it was lovely. And he survived and he thrived in there. It was absolutely fine, but just so vulnerable at that moment.

BOTTLEY Yeah, and there's that thing of, I remember, of being phoned by the hospital chaplain – they're amazing people – who'd baptized, because you're not supposed to baptize something that's not alive, obviously.

COLES Well, authorities conflict on this but never mind.

BOTTLEY But she'd phoned me up and said. 'I christened him. He was dead and I christened him.' And she went, 'And have you got a problem with that?' And I said, 'I've got no problem with that whatsoever.'

COLES Technically, wherever you think there might just be the remotest chance of the tiniest spark of life then you're okay.

BOTTLEY Well, then, I'm more than okay with it anyway but it's . . .

COLES I take a very liberal interpretation of that.

BOTTLEY Me too. But it's one of those things that catches your breath every now and again. And it happens all the time. In everything we do, we rock up to this stuff and it's just another day at the job and then every now and then you go – ooh, it's not just another day at the job, you know, this is somebody's baby, this is somebody's mum and this is the place where heaven touches earth. This is where we're the curators of the holy and we get complacent. I don't know about you, I can only speak for myself, but I get complacent about it just occasionally, and it's like God goes, 'Wake up, this is not just a thing, this is not just a job.'

COLES Our 10.30 a.m. is the most important day in that person's life and you have to remember it.

BOTTLEY And you have to remember that. And, God forgive me, but sometimes we occasionally think that it's about us, don't we?

COLES I don't know what you mean, Kate. Why are you directing that question at me?

BOTTLEY Why did I look directly at you when I said that, Richard?

FRASER My brother died in a cot death before I was born.
And that whole story about the vulnerability of young
kids, it just, like, permeates my family. And so, when
they arrive, I still have in the back of my head the absolute vulnerability of kids and that sort of need. It's part
of our, sort of, family psychology: the absolute need to
protect and so forth.

COLES You love a baby, though, Giles, don't you?

FRASER I just do.

BOTTLEY You adore a baby. Is it because you look a bit like
a baby?

COLES You know, but it's interesting that part of your family
narrative is the loss of your baby brother, and that's huge.

FRASER Yeah, yeah, it's huge, absolutely huge and he's in
my parents' garden. And it goes down the generations,
it absolutely echoes down the generations, and I'm sure
it totally dominates my approach to the way in which
I see birth.

BOTTLEY But we see that in the families that we minister
to. I mean, I was alongside a lady who was coming to the
end of her life who'd had a baby many years ago who'd
been stillborn, and in those days the baby was taken
away. She never held the baby, she never got . . . and all
she wanted on her deathbed was to find out where this
child was buried, and we couldn't – we weren't able to
do that for her. But we've all got stories like that, of that
generation of women and that generation of families
that never found out.

COLES One of the good things we do, and if you work with a charity like Sands, as I do, and you're able to hear that incredible, devastating, life-changing loss that people experience, which was previously kind of glossed over or seen as a sort of embarrassment in a backstory.

BOTTLEY Yeah. Have another one, you know, pick yourself up.

COLES I think people are much better about that now, aren't we? We used to do a carol service every year at St Paul's, and it was for Sands and it was for parents who had lost a child or a baby in the previous year; and it was incredibly moving, of course it was. But also, something about it's a carol service, songs about a child, a new baby that's just been born.

FRASER And that's exactly right. So, you're hearing all of these stories about the vulnerability of children and then you go into the Christmas story and the whole crazy idea that God may be born in a stable. It's easily the most . . .

COLES Vulnerable and tiny.

FRASER It's vulnerable and tiny. It's easily the most radical thing that Christianity ever dreamt up, the idea that God could be that vulnerable, that we might need to look after him. That's just absurd, you know, absolutely absurd. And it elicits from you, draws out of you, this compassion and concern. I'm sure that the elision of those two things at Christmas is so powerful.

BOTTLEY Yeah, but we can all agree that 'Away in a manger' is an awful hymn, right?

COLES But do you know what, Kate? I have to say it gets me that . . .

BOTTLEY You – I know you're a sentimental old fool, you love 'Away in a manger'.

COLES Well, no, it's not that. I mean, you know I don't have any children and the prospect of having any is vanishingly small. I've never looked after a baby, although I've looked after lots of babies, if you know what I mean. But I do find, as I get older in my late fifties now, 'Away in a manger' takes me right back to childhood and makes me have to sort of stop singing because . . .

BOTTLEY And I look forward to the day when I feel like that about it.

COLES And I am very sentimental, as I get older. I get more and more sentimental.

FRASER I like it too, actually, I like it too.

COLES It connects with something.

BOTTLEY Okay, I'm in a minority with 'Away in a manger'.

FRASER No, I like it too, I like it too.

COLES You do?

FRASER Yeah.

COLES Maybe we sentimentalize it and you don't because you've done it, Kate.

BOTTLEY Yeah, there's nothing sentimental about giving birth, it's just horrid.

COLES I would go for the elective caesarean, I think.

BOTTLEY Yeah, well I had an emergency caesarean twice.

COLES Right, well that's not so much fun, is it, the emergency part?

BOTTLEY No, it wasn't. Well, none of it was a lot of fun, but the feeding was good, I enjoyed that.

FRASER I mean there's also the fun stuff, the technical stuff about handling the baby.

BOTTLEY Oh, you see, well, because I ...

FRASER I love that now.

BOTTLEY ... well, you know, because I'm short and I can't see over the font at all, in any church I go in, because fonts aren't made for five-foot-tall women, I get the mum or dad to hold the baby and then we baptize together. So, they hold my hand under theirs and we all put the water on together. That's how we do it.

FRASER Have you ever had the most crazy list of names? Once I was asked to baptize the full list of Aston Villa Football Club.

BOTTLEY No!

FRASER Yes, the full list of the names. I backed off that one, actually. I didn't think that was quite ...

BOTTLEY I've not, but a friend of mine baptized a Smirnoff.

FRASER Really?

BOTTLEY Yeah, yeah, and we're not talking, like, some sort of Russian family name, kind of thing, you know, we are talking ... they called him Smirnoff Bailey, after their two favourite drinks.

COLES I've baptized a Saab.

BOTTLEY Have you?

COLES Yeah.

FRASER My two younger boys are Jewish, because my wife's Israeli. So, we had the rabbi to come round to do the circumcision, eighth day. So, I don't think this ceremony had ever happened in an Anglian vicarage . . . well, not in my Anglican vicarage before. So, he came down from Golders Green. And we did the ceremony. And the full shebang. And what I loved about that is that it was very close to the birth, so it had part of the drama of the birth that continued . . .

COLES The blood and guts.

FRASER Yes. And also that sort of very visceral nature of circumcision was, like – it was extraordinary and joining the part of that, you know, people of Israel at that point. And I'm the person then standing on the outside at this ceremony, as it were. I was the only non-Jew there present.

COLES Haven't you got Jewish heritage, Giles?

FRASER Yeah, my dad's Jewish but my mother's not, so I'm not halakhali Jewish.

BOTTLEY What are you asking him in that question?

COLES No, I just wondered how Jewish you were.

FRASER Yeah, well – oh no – well I was circumcised . . .

COLES That's not what I was asking.

FRASER Oh, I see. Oh well, I was circumcised by the mohel at Golders Green on the dining-room table. But my kids, they're halakhali Jewish, my two younger ones, so it was the full ceremony. And it was really peculiar to do it in the vicarage. Really nice, really, really nice.

COLES But baptisms, though: I pride myself on my baby-handling, which I think's pretty good.

BOTTLEY So, where do you go? Do you go head . . .

COLES Head there . . .

BOTTLEY Head in the crook of your arm . . .

COLES Cradled like that; dip over . . .

BOTTLEY Right.

COLES Then we have the eighteenth-century baptism gift of St John English Dalbane? Da, da, da, da . . .

BOTTLEY Yes, of course.

COLES Splish, splosh, splish, splosh. And then I get one of the children to dab any drips. So I get children to assist and then . . .

BOTTLEY Okay. I did one for a very lively toddler on Easter Day once and the parents were very worried – because the parents are always worried about the baby crying and you being able to hold the baby. That's what I found; those are the sort of main concerns. And we ended up with super-soakers and just had a massive water fight on the church lawn instead, and that was it. And I've never sort of blessed a super-soaker before.

FRASER Blessed a what?

COLES It's a gun, a water pistol.

BOTTLEY A water pistol.

COLES You know, those – the ones you pump up.

BOTTLEY Those punchy ones. So, we just did that for the christening.

COLES You'd love them.

BOTTLEY You would love that.

FRASER You didn't?

BOTTLEY Yeah, we did.

COLES Don't look at me. I'm kosher, mate.

FRASER I'm shocked.

BOTTLEY There was no way of getting that child wet other than doing that. But we – you put, like, a rubber duck in the font, right?

COLES No.

BOTTLEY No? Oh, I do.

COLES And that's all fine, isn't it?

FRASER I'm really shocked.

BOTTLEY Throw a rubber duck in the font.

COLES You mean sacramentally?

FRASER You don't, do you?

BOTTLEY Yeah, of course I do. Because then the baby looks down, especially if it's an older child, which invariably it is these days. We don't do that whole 'babies are christened quick before they die' kind of thing, do we? We don't tend to do that these days; they're sort of one-year-olds, right?

COLES That's funny you say that because in my church we have the wall of tears, which is the north wall, and if you dig there you very often turn up the bones of babies who would have been clandestinely buried in the churchyard. I'm sure, and I hope and I pray, with the active connivance and support of the vicar in the days when unbaptized babies were not considered . . .

BOTTLEY Weren't allowed to be buried.

COLES Yeah, but of course they all were.

BOTTLEY Well, and my mum wasn't allowed in my grand-mother's house, you know, bearing in mind I'm not that old, my mum was not allowed over the threshold of my grandmother's until she was churched – we were not allowed in.

COLES Really?

BOTTLEY No, we were still churching the women; my mum was churched.

COLES I've never been to a churching of women.

BOTTLEY Have you not?

COLES No.

BOTTLEY My mum was churched. And when my babies were born, the first outing they had was to church. My first outing, after my babies were born, was to go to church.

COLES So, even though it wasn't the rite from the Book of Common Prayer . . .

BOTTLEY No, it wasn't the . . .

COLES . . . it was a tradition that endured?

BOTTLEY Yeah, absolutely, that's what you do, even in my non-church family.

COLES Presentation.

FRASER We should explain what churching of women is.

BOTTLEY We should explain what churching of women is.

FRASER So, the idea, I guess the idea is that somehow when you give birth you are unclean, in some ways, which would be something in the Hebrew Scriptures . . .

COLES The mikvah, wouldn't it?

74

BOTTLEY Yeah.

FRASER And that you require some sort of cleansing. Now, that's quite complicated theologically because there are two sorts of – it's not a sinful thing. Not all forms of uncleanliness are sinful. That often gets elided but it's actually a ritual form of uncleanliness, which is not sort of . . .

BOTTLEY My grandmother wouldn't have any woman over her threshold that hadn't been churched after she'd given birth.

COLES Really? Not stepping over my threshold.

BOTTLEY No, not stepping over – not asked. And despite the fact that she didn't go to church herself.

COLES We have a record at my church of a woman who had been found in adultery, who was made to present herself to church – this was in the early nineteenth century – and be sort of denounced and then forgiven formally, publicly. That was a thing. Imagine that.

BOTTLEY Imagine that.

FRASER What I particularly love . . .

BOTTLEY But not the man that she committed adultery with, presumably?

COLES No.

BOTTLEY Mmm, patriarchy.

FRASER What I love about baptism is that you get this idea about the relationship between blood and water because . . .

COLES The floating Christ sign.

FRASER Well, the idea that, in a way, for Christianity water's thicker than blood. So, when you get baptized, you're a part of the church family and then this is the way in which you're part of this new family – reborn into this new family. And water is what binds you together, not blood. There's this fantastic thing that they do – took me ages to work out why they did it – everybody was calling each other auntie and uncle in my church, everybody did it. I thought there was about two families in my church to start with. But actually, the big West African tradition is that we're all related in baptism and so we're all called aunties and uncles.

BOTTLEY Same in the North. Same in Yorkshire.

FRASER I hadn't come across it before. But it's absolutely right. And so, you have this whole idea of the family of the Church, which is bound together through baptism, and especially when you have a very multicultural church like mine. It's a fantastic symbol, in a way, that blood becomes parochial, you know.

COLES We're very monocultural where I am, although we do have a traveller community and sometimes you get traveller baptism. The thing that's most striking about that, and I think it's because people have their kids very young, you'll quite often have a baptism when you've got five generations round the font, which I've never known before in any other circumstances. So, literally, five generations at the font. And you get a real sense there about this being not just belonging to the parents and the child and the godparents, but to the wider community too. Big thing. And water's big because they always like to take away holy water, water from the font, in a bottle, and take it home.

We have this thing, as well. Now, as you know, I'm a person of extraordinary physical bravery and . . .

BOTTLEY Mmm, it has been said.

COLES When we took the parish on a pilgrimage to the Holy Land and the River Jordan, the bit where Jesus is reputed to have been baptized by John, I went down to the river and under the gaze of the Israeli Defence Force on one side and the Jordanian Army on the other side I got a bottle of Jordan water to take home, and we use a drop of that in the font.

BOTTLEY Isn't that what the royal family do? They're baptized in Jordan water, aren't they?

COLES They may have copied that . . .

BOTTLEY I think they've copied it.

FRASER We do that as well. [laughter]

BOTTLEY The good folk at Finedon. We don't, we just use corporation wine, that's what we use.

COLES Over the years it has perhaps become a little diluted, but nonetheless.

BOTTLEY Have you been topping it up from the cold tap, Father?

COLES No, from the font. But it's the symbolism, isn't it? It's that idea that what you're doing is baptizing somebody into something that's been going . . .

BOTTLEY In my last church I had to replace the – so we've got this kind of, like, twelfth-century font thing.

COLES Twelfth-century font thing!

BOTTLEY I'm so sorry. The plug doesn't really work on it, so you can't just pull the plug out and the water goes away. So, instead, you had a Tupperware fruit bowl inside that you put the water in, which I did replace with a nice glass, cut glass crystal one.

COLES I've got a lovely, really nice faceted bowl by a significant contemporary potter.

BOTTLEY Of course you have. That you had to get a mortgage out to pay for.

COLES No, no, no.

BOTTLEY Okay, here's a niche question: what's your favourite font? Not Comic Sans, obviously.

COLES No, I really would say – mine.

BOTTLEY Your own font?

COLES Yeah.

BOTTLEY Salisbury Cathedral.

COLES Oh, lovely.

BOTTLEY Oh, great font, beautiful. Have you got a favourite font?

FRASER No, I don't have a favourite.

BOTTLEY Made me want to have another baby. When I saw Salisbury's font for the first time I was, like, that's it, I'm going to breed again.

FRASER My church was destroyed in the war and rebuilt. In fact, lots of the churches that I've been at have been burnt and rebuilt.

BOTTLEY Are you not setting a pattern, Giles?

FRASER No, well – I wasn't there for the Great Fire of London. You can't pin that one on me. [*laughter*]

COLES So, that's why you left St Paul's.

FRASER But the new church, where I am now, is smaller than the old one, and where the plate at the font is – still outside – there's a cross where the old font was. And I've always wanted to try and build something on that spot to mark, maybe a fountain or something like that, just to mark the site where it was. And it was in the right place, where you come into the church, so you come into the church through the baptism.

BOTTLEY Yeah, because that's the symbolism we lose, isn't it, on reorganizing the churches when we move the font to the front?

COLES Yeah, don't do that.

BOTTLEY Don't do that.

COLES The other thing that's great about the font is that people gather there; that's the draw, isn't it? When I was at St Paul's, Knightsbridge, because it was quite posh, I remember once – I'm a big Arsenal fan – and I was doing . . .

FRASER [*sigh*]

COLES I'm sorry. Chelsea man, aren't you? Appalling . . .

BOTTLEY Is this football, is it?

COLES Call yourself a Christian! Anyway, there I was at the font, baptizing, and I looked up at one of the godfathers, and it was Tony Adams, and I literally went . . . [*speechless noises*]

BOTTLEY That's like when I met Kylie.

COLES Practically dropped the baby on the floor. [*losing it noises*] You're Tony Adams, I really like you. [*laughter*]

BOTTLEY I like you.

COLES I like you; I think you're really good. And they're saying, 'Get on with it.' And I'm, 'Yeah, whatever. I really miss you in the back four.'

FRASER My problem is that, in terms of what I have in my head, is I find it very difficult when I say, 'Do you turn to Christ?' 'I turn to Christ.' 'Do you repent of your sins?' 'I repent of my sins.' 'Do you renounce evil?' 'I renounce evil.' I just can't help but think about *The Godfather*. I mean, I'm doing the baptism and there's that scene where everybody gets shot in *The Godfather*, that absolutely brilliant scene, and I'm trying to be holy and I'm just getting the idea of people getting machine gunned.

BOTTLEY But I get them to actually turn, at that point, so I get them to face west and then turn towards the cross at that point.

COLES I've always felt awkward if somebody says, 'Actually, no, I don't renounce evil.'

FRASER No, that's . . . no, no, that's happened, that's happened at a church in Oxfordshire, and there was this little lad that was mic'd up, and he was obviously old enough to answer questions for himself but he was – I don't know – eight or something like that and the priest said, 'Do you turn to Christ?' And a little voice went, 'No.' And then there was a sort of, like – the microphone went down, Mother had a word, the microphone went back on again: 'Do you turn to Christ?' 'Yes.' [*laughter*]

BOTTLEY But that's the downside of christening older children, because you have to ask them, don't you? The rubric says if they're of age you have to say to them, 'Is it your wish to be baptized?' And there's that awful moment when you go, 'Is it your wish to be baptized?' And they sort of go, 'Yeeaaah.'

FRASER I think the interesting thing about that story about the little boy, that people who are listening would think that's why you need to be old enough to make a decision for yourself – and the people who have problems with infant baptism and so forth. But I have no problem with infant baptism whatsoever. It's just giving people the sort of background against which things make sense.

BOTTLEY I remember when we had our children baptized in quite an evangelical church and there was a lot of people who didn't. And my thing was, I decide everything for them – I decide what they wear; I decide what they eat; I decide when they go to bed – why wouldn't I decide the most important thing?

COLES But they are in their thirties now, Kate. [*laughter*]

BOTTLEY How old do you think I am? So rude. Why do I like you as much as I do?

FRASER But isn't there that wonderful thing, that absolutely wonderful thing? This is what I love the best. Maybe this is to do with my family story when people have tried hard to have a child and haven't had one and then suddenly they've had one and they come to the church, bringing their child. They're so proud, they're so excited, this is just the most astonishing, beautiful, wonderful day, and you can see it on their faces just how proud and delighted they are.

BOTTLEY And they bring with them twenty-eight god-parents because they couldn't possibly choose – that's the ones I like.

COLES Godparents, have you been one, are you one? You must be . . .

BOTTLEY I am, yeah, yeah. Five, I've got.

COLES Giles?

FRASER Probably quite a lot more than that, but I don't know, I can't remember.

BOTTLEY What do you mean, you don't know?

FRASER I've lost count.

COLES Have you lost the certificates?

FRASER What certificates?

COLES Exactly. [*laughter*]

BOTTLEY Are you not issuing certificates?

FRASER Well, no, no, I actually issue certificates but obviously the baptisms that I've been to . . .

BOTTLEY Right.

FRASER . . . I might have been given them . . .

BOTTLEY Okay.

FRASER . . . I don't keep them.

COLES I forgot I was my nephew's godfather until my brother reminded me. But my godchildren are now sort of grown up. Two of them have graduated from university, one only last week, and I've been part of that.

FRASER So, what – these days when you're choosing them, so what people do, I think, is they go, what we need as a godparent is we need a rich one, we need a funny one, we need a religious one . . .

COLES And a gay one.

FRASER . . . and we need a gay one. And one of them that you can talk to when you get into trouble about drugs or sex when you're about sixteen.

COLES That's the gay one.

BOTTLEY But it sounds like Richard . . . [*laughter*] . . . it sounds like you've got it covered then: you've got all those categories, haven't you?

COLES Well, I've had to turn down now because I didn't think . . .

FRASER You're probably the perfect godfather, aren't you?

BOTTLEY You've turned them down?

COLES I say I'm sorry, I just can't – I can't . . .

BOTTLEY How do you turn down . . .

FRASER You're the religious one, you're the gay one, you're the rich one . . .

BOTTLEY Funny one.

FRASER The funny one – you've got the lot. You are the perfect godfather, Richard Coles.

COLES The formerly rich one. Yeah, no, no. Because I want to take it seriously, I couldn't take on any more than I did. So, I said, 'Really nice to be asked but I'm afraid

I just can't, I couldn't do it justice.' If you're a clergy person you're quite likely to get asked . . .

FRASER Yes.

BOTTLEY Yeah, yeah.

COLES . . . because you have the most significant qualifier . . .

FRASER I'm a terrible godfather. I apologize to all my god-children, I really do.

BOTTLEY Why are you terrible? Do you not pray for them?

FRASER Yeah. I can't remember their names often, so that's like . . .

BOTTLEY That's all right, God knows their names.

FRASER . . . that's, like, I've got loads and . . .

COLES Hello, Giles, I'm your goddaughter.

FRASER Yes, I know. I apologize to all of you and I love you very much and I'm really sorry.

COLES For me, intention is everything, and in that moment people want the best for that child. That's enough for me. Let's work to address that – people want the best for this child.

FRASER But the sacramental viability of the baptism is not in the slightest bit dependent upon the intention of the godparents . . .

BOTTLEY Or on us, thank God, or on the priest – on our efficacy.

FRASER Absolutely, exactly right.

COLES But there is something significant about intention, and you find this when people come to us because they know other people, for thousands of years, hundreds of years, have brought kids, brought the dead, brought their young people – you know, to get married, to get hatched and matched and dispatched, and even if the theology is remote and if they would never come to church for any other reason, if they don't know a hymn or the Lord's Prayer, there's still something in that that's powerful.

BOTTLEY Yeah, and that's the conversation, isn't it, the conversation where you go into people's homes and you meet in the pub to talk about the baptism of their baby, and you go, 'Why do you want your child christened?' They say, 'I don't really know. I just do, it feels proper, it feels right, I want to do it properly.' I had a woman who'd had several children taken into care. This was a most recent baby, and the others had not been baptized and she just said to me, 'I want to get it right this time.' And having that baby baptized was part of her framework of getting it right this time.

FRASER We're so lucky doing what we do. I think that's the point where I feel most privileged, actually – the baptism.

BOTTLEY Have you had vomit in a font yet?

FRASER No, I haven't.

COLES You have, haven't you?

BOTTLEY I've had vomit.

COLES Did you reverently dispose of it?

BOTTLEY No, I scooped – I scooped and flicked. It was the only thing I could do, really.

COLES Do you know what I think? Correct me if I'm wrong but I think one of the things that's happened with our discussions is that *you* love baptisms, *you* love weddings and *I* love funerals.

FRASER I think that's true.

BOTTLEY We're like a dream package.

FRASER That's true, actually.

COLES Crap at two things and good at one. [*laughter*]

BOTTLEY That's the other way of seeing it.

FRASER That is absolutely – that's actually just come out, hasn't it?

COLES We are a trinity of sacramental offering.

FRASER Absolutely, yeah, that's absolutely right.

BOTTLEY It's only because I like the shoes.

FRASER Of course, a baptism's the most theologically rich of the . . .

COLES Of course, the funeral is the most theologically rich . . .

BOTTLEY Of course the wedding is . . . [*laughter*]

FRASER But this is where – the baptism is where you enter into the body of Christ. You're reborn . . .

COLES The funeral's where you go into the mystery of God.

BOTTLEY And weddings have really good canapes and champagne. [*laughter*] And I get to wear nice shoes.

COLES Well, of course, nothing unleashes like the tongues of three vicars talking shop. It's been such a lovely time to talk to Giles Fraser and Kate Bottley, and to be Richard Coles having that conversation with all the three of us. Thanks very much. Let's do it again.

FRASER Let's do it again.

COLES Bottley?

BOTTLEY It's your round, I think, ain't it?

COLES What does that mean?

BOTTLEY Oh, it's fine, don't worry. Just consecrate the communion wine, it'll be fine.

Music: 'Isn't She Lovely' by Stevie Wonder

Christmas

Broadcast on Christmas Day 2019, at 1.15 p.m.

Presenters:	RICHARD COLES KATE BOTTLEY GILES FRASER
Producer:	NEIL MORROW
Series editor:	CHRISTINE MORGAN
Music:	'I Wish it Could be Christmas Every Day' by Slade

COLES I wish it could be Christmas every day. Now that's not a phrase that drops very commonly from the lips of clergy towards the end of the year. I'm joined by two colleagues: by the Reverend Kate Bottley and the Reverend Canon Giles Fraser. All of us have form when it comes to Christmas but I'm wondering, Kate, there's something about you that suggests to me that a pair of novelty antlers would work for you. Do you love Christmas?

BOTTLEY Umm... Oh, there was too much of a pause there really, wasn't there? To not tell the truth – no.

FRASER [*sharp intake of breath*]

COLES [*sharp intake of breath*]

BOTTLEY I know. Okay. Let me explain. I love Christmas; I love the actual day itself because, I don't know about you two, but actually by Christmas it's all done. Christmas Day, after about 11 o'clock or so, you've got nothing else, unless you've got a church that is dedicated to St Stephen. So, you can pretty much kick back and relax – or that Christmas Day is on a Saturday...

COLES Which does happen.

BOTTLEY ... which is the worst thing in the world for a clergyperson. I love Christmas. What I find really tricky is that we peak too soon, as far as I'm concerned. So, as clergy...

FRASER When you say 'we', do you mean church?

BOTTLEY No, I don't. I mean those people that we're here to serve. So, for me [*laughing*], the thing that really gets me, okay – I'm going to really nail this down – I don't like people who take their Christmas trees down on Boxing Day. That's what upsets me.

COLES Would you last till Candlemas?

BOTTLEY Yeah, absolutely; till February, definitely.

COLES How about you? When does the greenery – you don't put greenery up, do you, Giles?

FRASER No, no, no, I like – I love the Christmas tree. So, about three years ago I asked my daughter and kids if they would decorate the Christmas tree, and that was a big mistake because my daughter was at Goldsmiths, the fine art college, and so she decided – and I let them do it in the day – and when I came back, my daughter had spray painted tampons and had used those as Christmas decorations. And when the ladies of the parish came in to look at the vicar's Christmas tree it took some explanation.

COLES Well, it invites a very interesting parish discussion on the virgin birth perhaps, doesn't it? [*laughter*]

FRASER I love Christmas. I sort of even love secular Christmas, I have to say. I sort of pooh-pooh it a bit. I love the whole mood and the sort of drawing in, wintery type of thing, and the way that's sort of taken up by . . .

COLES Do you have a bit of hygge in Newington Butts?

FRASER That sort of thing, yeah, we light a fire. And when I was at St Paul's at Christmas it was a sort of industrial thing, you know: you had to do thirty carol services and I was absolutely sick of it by the end of it. But the great thing about where I am now is that I only have a few carol services, so I absolutely love them.

BOTTLEY Well, this is exactly my point: it's actually not Christmas that's the problem, is it? It's the run-up to it. You know when it comes to the Dibley episode where she has eight Christmas dinners in a day? That, as far as I'm concerned, is a documentary, it's not a drama. I remember on my fourth Christmas dinner one week, because the schools all have their Christmas dinners on the same day. So if you've got a few schools in your parish, you end up having to have four Christmas dinners, that's actually true. And there's only so much enthusiasm you can muster for 'Away in a manger' again, right? So, you're sat next to somebody who's going, 'Ooh, ain't it lovely?' 'No, it's hideous.'

COLES I mean, I find I'm sort of conflicted about it because on the one hand I was in a church before Finedon, in Knightsbridge, again we did thirty carol services and, to be honest, 'Hark the herald angels sing', two goes is plenty for me; thirty goes is awful.

BOTTLEY Are you having a bash at the descant, Father?

COLES No – well, I have a theory about that. You know how spider plants and cockroaches are the only things that survive a nuclear explosion? I think the descant to 'O little town of Bethlehem' will as well! There is something, isn't there, about Midnight Mass and 'O Little town of Bethlehem' and people, creaky old sopranos, remembering from childhood the descant – [*singing*] 'Oh holy child' . . .

BOTTLEY You see, I really like it. I really like that because I can't do the descant, so I try really hard to do it, just so that people turn . . .

FRASER And it's heresy, by the way, that hymn. Shouldn't be allowed: 'veiled in flesh the Godhead see' – it's not a veiling, it's the real thing, he's a person . . .

BOTTLEY Who put sixpence in Giles?

FRASER I know. So, it's like, we should ban that hymn for heresy.

COLES You don't preach that Christmas sermon which pooh-poohs Father Christmas, do you?

FRASER No, I don't. I do have the sort of – you know, we all have a number of different Christmas sermons but they all sort of converge on one and my Christmas sermon usually involves finding someone in the congregation with a baby.

BOTTLEY Yeah, I do that one. That makes them cry every time.

FRASER And you get the baby . . .

COLES So obvious, soo obvious . . . cliché.

BOTTLEY Makes them cry every single time.

FRASER You do, don't you? Of course. [*laughter*]

BOTTLEY Yeah, the baby at the back of the carol service. The people that you never see have just had a baby, so they've brought the baby for Christmas for the first time . . . and you go to the back and you go, 'Halfway through this sermon I'm going to come over and nick your baby. Is that all right?' And they go, 'Yeah that's fine.' So, you stand at the front and you go – 'You know, what is it really all about? You know, is it about the tree? Is it about the presents? Is it about the . . .' And then you go, 'No, it's about this.' And you walk down the silent church, down the aisle, collect the baby and bring it to the front and hold it, and there's not a dry eye in the house.

FRASER And you say this is what God looks like.

BOTTLEY That's it, that's what you do, just crank it up. I don't let them leave church until they've cried; that's how it works.

COLES I don't think my Midnight Mass sermon is preached until I've spoken about the child that is born to die.

BOTTLEY [*laughing*] I've got a Christmas jumper with that on, got a picture of the nativity on it and it says, 'Spoiler alert, he dies'. It's my favourite.

FRASER Oooh.

COLES The conflict for me, you know: there are methods of handling that. My first parish, lovely vicar there, my training incumbent, and we used to do lots of carol services there, and it had beautiful medieval choir stalls. So, we'd come in at the beginning, together, robed, coped, blah, blah, blah, hello everybody, and then you could lean back in the stall. But what they didn't know, there was a little gate at the back of the stall: you could go out; we could go to the vicarage. And so we'd have a whisky, and then the verger could ring a bell when it was 'Hark the herald' and we'd just come back in . . .

FRASER No!

COLES Yeah, just reappear for 'Hark the herald' . . .

BOTTLEY I love that.

COLES . . . And we'd sing. And that was a lifesaver, actually. I love Christmas, and I love Christmas because I think it's the thing that most securely and powerfully and poignantly connects me to childhood and the expectations of childhood.

BOTTLEY Okay, who were you in the nativity play?

COLES You touch on an awkward and difficult point, Kate, because I really, really wanted to be a king, but I was a shepherd.

BOTTLEY Would you like me to do the pastoral head tilt at you because you're touching into deep childhood trauma here?

FRASER Do you have people turning up for your nativity, like I had one year where the little boy turns up as Batman, okay, for the nativity play, and you think, Oh we'll find a way of getting you in . . . [laughing]

BOTTLEY Oh, my favourite thing with the nativity play in church is to do the scratch nativity. So, to stop any arguments about who's going to be Mary and who's going to be the Angel Gabriel, and all that sort of stuff – Narrator One by the way – what we'd do is just have a big box of dressing-up clothes and you'd just go at the beginning of the service and the kids and grown-ups would just leg it to the dressing-up box and whoever got the costume first, that was what part they played.

FRASER Is that what you do?

BOTTLEY Yeah.

COLES Mmm – that makes me think of the man at the pool of Bethesda, but never mind.

FRASER The problem with Christmas is this – this is my theological sort of two penn'orth – is that we have this sort of sentimental view of it but it's actually the most radical festival, sort of, theologically ever invented: the idea that God – the thing that almost all cultures imagine to be power and transcendence – becomes powerless and immanent. And I think we've, sort of, lost how shocking Christmas is amongst all the tinsel. That's the bit that gets me.

COLES It is nonetheless durable. I mean, I was a chorister when I was a kid, so I grew up with it all, but as soon as I could get out of it I did, with a kind of full-bloodied atheism and a commitment to a material world. But the thing that endured through all that was Christmas, actually, and I would creep back to Midnight Mass, just to kind of touch base with it again, because it was important to me and because I kind of sensed in it something that was enduring and powerful and radical and spoke to that radicalness.

BOTTLEY I grew up with none of that. I went to church of my own volition when I was fourteen . . .

COLES Where do you come from, weirdo?

BOTTLEY I fancied the vicar's son – you know that; you know that story.

COLES Yeah, you married him.

BOTTLEY Later, I married him. Anyway, we were never taken to church, so we never had any of that. It was all Father Christmas; it was all Coca-Cola trucks; it had nothing to do with Jesus – Christmas – really. I mean we said grace occasionally around the table on Christmas Day. That was only once I'd got religion, though.

COLES Did you have a religious Advent calendar or did you have chocolate Advent . . .

BOTTLEY Chocolate Advent calendar. There's no other sort – I still do. I've just been into the gift shop here at St Martin's to see if they'd got any Advent calendars. They've only got the rubbish religious ones with Jesus on, no chocolate in. What's that?

FRASER Raise it with the rector.

BOTTLEY What's that!

COLES I think one of the things that's sometimes difficult for clergy is that our churches are often full, fuller than they are at any other time of year, but we don't always connect in the way we think we connect with the people who are there, do we? Does it bother you that you can find a Christmas stamp and there's nothing Christian on it? Or does it bother you that there are Christmas cards for sale and it's all Santas and reindeer?

FRASER I sort of love both, actually. I love the sort of culture of schmaltzy sentimental Christmas because I'm schmaltzy and sentimental myself. The only thing I don't like about it is the way it obscures something of the clarity of what's going on theologically with Christmas, which is much more radical, much more shocking than people think.

BOTTLEY Have you ever done the – I've got a sermon for you, then – have you ever done the manger covered in tinsel sermon where you hide the manger under a pile of baubles and tinsel and then you get the kids to try and find the baby Jesus underneath all the tinsel?

FRASER Oh, very nice.

BOTTLEY There you go, you see; you can have that one.

COLES I wanted an iPad!

BOTTLEY [*laughing*] But it's the myths and the legends around it, because that's what happens – you get a church full of people who think they know what Christmas is, right? So, I wrote an article for *Saga Magazine*, which no doubt you read, Richard [*laughter*] . . . I wrote an article for *Saga Magazine* last year about Christmas and wrote about how there is no mention of the donkey, there is no mention of three kings, certainly the shepherds and the Magi weren't at the same place at the same time. Well, the letters I got! You would not believe how angry people were. There was one woman who went, 'Of course there was a donkey. What about the carol "Little donkey"?' I don't think that was written in . . .

COLES The first sermon, the first sermon I ever preached was a Christmas sermon, and I preached to say that the reason Christ was born at Bethlehem was to do with prophecy in the Old Testament, and a voice rose from the wife of a retired canon at the back and she went, 'Rubbish.'

FRASER Oh, really.

COLES That was my first ever sermon feedback.

FRASER I've just come back from Israel for three months and I went to Bethlehem. I was in Bethlehem a few weeks ago and I always have the same problem when I go there, and it's sort of part of the problem I have with Christmas, which is that people get on the bus from Jerusalem and they come in really, really quickly, and they get out of the bus – air-conditioned buses – and they go straight into the fancy church and it's, sort of, like, you know, this is where Jesus was born. And then they get back on to the bus, and they leg it and they don't really see the wider – like in Bethlehem there's lots of Christians and it's quite difficult . . .

COLES In Manger Square, of course, there were tanks not that long ago.

FRASER Exactly right. And the whole idea of the sort of living stones of the people of the Church, rather than the sort of fancy stones. And it's the sort of tinsel churchiness that can sometimes obscure it all.

COLES And that connects us to what you were saying. That there's, I think, the reason why Christmas, even if it does seem to be completely lost behind the kind of gloss of tinsel or the kind of sentimentality of adverts with fire-breathing dragons in, is that it does connect you to that really powerful idea. And I still think the reason why people still connect to that is because it is ineradicably powerful, this sense that God has become flesh.

BOTTLEY   And it's one of us, the image of Mary and that; a woman with low status becomes the person who carries the Christ child. That was always really a powerful image for me, even as an Evangelical-heritage girl there was always a really powerful metaphor in that image of Mary holding that baby.

COLES   But we're all High Church at Christmas, aren't we?

BOTTLEY   Yeah, of course we are.

COLES   There's something about Christmas that is just High Church.

FRASER   Yeah, it is.

BOTTLEY   Of course, of course you want candles, you want handbags on fire, you want all that.

COLES   What about Advent? You see, Advent is my favourite season. Invidious to our faith, but it is my favourite season of the Church's year. The music is lovely: it's all French and in G minor and dark and bitter, and I love all that. But also . . .

BOTTLEY   Not in my church, it isn't.

COLES   . . . but it's the preparation, it's like Lent before Easter, isn't it? It's this sort of period of leanness before you hit the feast; there's something about light coming to you in darkness that's really . . .

BOTTLEY   Do you actually fast in Advent, then?

COLES   Kind of, yeah. I only have a blended whisky not a malt. [*laughter*]

FRASER You see, I'm something of a heretic on this. I do think of Advent as Christmas in waiting, so it does have Christmas qualities to it. So, when . . .

COLES Anticipation.

FRASER Absolutely. In terms of anticipation, but sort of semi-realization: it's coming. I don't like the idea that the clergy are always sort of terribly mean-spirited about the anticipation of Christmas. I mean, it used to be the case; I think no clergy really do this any more – there'll be absolutely no whiff of any Christmassy sort of music, or very puritan in the lead-up to Christmas.

COLES You just can't do that, though, not if you're Church of England.

BOTTLEY But you must have someone in your church that complains that the crib's gone up too early and that the trees have gone up too early. We had a woman in one of my churches who used to get really angry about Christmas trees in church because they were pagan. And I tried to explain to her that if you took everything that was pagan out of Christianity there wouldn't be a lot left, to be fair. But she weren't having that, she was like – you would come to church and she would have dragged the tree out the front door again, and you would be dragging it back in.

COLES At Finedon we have an Advent carol service, a Christmas carol service and an Epiphany carol service, and it's always interesting to plot between those three points where everybody else is. Advent carol service, people say, 'Why couldn't we have "O little town of Bethlehem"?' and you think, well, it's not Christmas yet. Christmas everybody gets that. Epiphany, they're thinking – what are you talking about?

BOTTLEY We've done this, I'm glad it's all over. That's my point, that's the tree down on Boxing Day. Especially, as clergy, we've had this marathon up to the big day itself, so just when we're ready to pop the champagne corks and get our glad rags on, everybody else is going, 'Oh, I'm glad that's over.' You know, my mother's took her tree down.

FRASER There's a really interesting class alignment of which service you go to. It strikes me that Midnight Mass is generally a pretty middle-class thing to do – that's where I am. Now, I'm not in a middle-class parish; Christmas Day is really, really big, Midnight Mass not so much. I'm really quite interested in that.

COLES Because I'm in a sort of mixed parish, but Midnight Mass is our biggest service of the year.

FRASER Really?

COLES And Christmas Day is when the farmers come. So, the farming families come all in Sunday best, it's a tradition. They come, and then everybody goes to the cemetery and the graveyard to visit the graves . . .

BOTTLEY Yeah, that's where we – that's where we used to go.

FRASER They go to the cemetery and the graveyard for what?

COLES To visit the graves of their dead.

BOTTLEY Yeah, that's what we do Christmas Day. We never went to church, as kids, on Christmas Day, ever, we never went to church. But we used to go to the graveyard.

COLES You talk about this because you didn't grow up in an explicitly religious family, but it seems to me that it was a family in which all those traditions were observed. I've heard you talk about it before.

BOTTLEY Yeah, we used to all meet at Christmas Day at the graveside of my nan nan and my – that's grandmother to you . . .

COLES Thank you.

BOTTLEY . . . nan nan and – me nan nan and grandad – and leave flowers, and all that sort of stuff, and that was our little ritual, kind of thing; that's what we did. So, it was really weird because that's one of the things, ain't it, when you get together with your life partners and stuff, you have to sort of figure out where your traditions are. And one of the first stand-up arguments me and Graham had, when we were first together, was where you spend Christmas morning, because for him it wasn't Christmas unless you were in church being miserable. And that thing is showing your presence.

FRASER It's not miserable. Why is it miserable?

BOTTLEY Because everybody wants to get out of there as quickly as possible, Giles.

FRASER Why?

BOTTLEY Because there's turkey to be having.

FRASER I thought you didn't like turkey. I thought you just said you had too much of it.

BOTTLEY No, no, no.

COLES David, my partner, who was born and raised half in the north and half in the south, he loves all those traditions. So, we have a thing: like other clergy, of course, we have Midnight Mass and then we have an eight o'clock in the morning. We've been probably really busy in the run-up, you're a bit tired.

BOTTLEY The first thing I did in parish was cancel that eight o'clock.

COLES Did you?

BOTTLEY Yeah, if you've got a vicar with a family, we're still opening presents at that time.

FRASER Yeah.

BOTTLEY There's no way that's happening.

COLES But David does stockings for the dogs, right, we've got five dogs . . .

BOTTLEY Does he have opposable thumbs?

COLES He does stockings for the dogs, so, after I come home from Midnight Mass all I want to do is go to bed, but then we have to fill the dogs' stockings but the dogs can't be in the room because it will spoil the surprise. [*laughter*] Seriously. So, there I am, haggard with fatigue, and he's going, 'Don't show them . . . don't let them see,' as we do the dogs' stockings. And then I have to get up at six o'clock, and then he insists on having smoked salmon, caviar and champagne for breakfast, which is very nice but I just really need to go to work. Do you know what I mean? And then that thing that's really interesting: once we're done, which is usually by midday, then . . .

FRASER You sleep, don't you, then?

COLES Well, I actually get into pyjamas and watch *The Sound of Music*.

FRASER No!

COLES Yeah, pyjamas and *Sound of Music*.

FRASER You get into pyjamas and you watch *The Sound of Music*?

COLES Yeah, and we eat.

BOTTLEY I want to think about that as a mental picture for a moment. One of my clergy friends, what she does is she buys the biggest takeaway she can on Christmas Eve, at the latest slot that the curry house will deliver it, and then she takes it out of the bags and puts it in the fridge and that's her Christmas lunch for the day after – ping and ding, straight in the microwave, that'll do.

COLES Do you think people would be disappointed if they thought that clergy were not actually embodying in every breath the sort of spirit of Dickensian Christmas?

BOTTLEY Well, you summed it up there, didn't you, because you said, actually I just want to get to work. Although it's a vocation, although it's a privilege, although it's a calling, although it's all those things, actually part of it is a job as well.

COLES But then it's that beautiful thing, isn't it? That beautiful thing with the star. At our church, we have everyone in, jammed for Midnight Mass. Everyone's drunk from the pub, da, da, da, and then it's completely dark; we switch all the lights off and the only light is at the crib. And we have the reading, the Prologue to the Gospel of John.

BOTTLEY Gets me every time.

COLES Me too.

FRASER Me too, me too.

BOTTLEY So, the moment for me: in all my cynicism, in all my grumpiness, in all my Scrooge-like behaviour; in all my 'oh no we've peaked too soon; I'm not eating any more sprouts; oh my word, "Away in the manger" is the worse song ever invented' . . . Oh, come on, don't look at me like that, Giles, it's hideous.

FRASER I love it.

BOTTLEY Oh, man.

FRASER Oh, I love it.

BOTTLEY Do you know what, I already had quite a low opinion of you but now it's just gone down even further . . .

FRASER I love it.

COLES Kate, there's something you need to know.

BOTTLEY What? You love it too?

COLES I love it too.

BOTTLEY Oh my . . . shock!

COLES You have to drag it out of me, but it's true: I do.

BOTTLEY The moment for me is after Midnight Mass when I walk out into the empty churchyard and I can hear them all doing their handshakes and doing all the merry Christmases, and I always made sure I would stand alone in that churchyard and look at the sky. And that's it, that's the moment for me when I go, I don't have to sing 'Away in a manger' again. I don't have to do all that, I don't have to – the tree's up, the presents . . . If it's not done by now, it's never going to get done. And that's the moment, that's the moment of Christmas. And I just look at it and I cannot help but sob. And in my last parish there used to be a farmer at that point, who would sidle up to me and go, 'All right, Vicar?' And I'd go, 'Yeah.' And he'd go, 'Whisky?' 'Yes, please, that would be lovely.' And he'd just pass me the hip flask and leave it with me.

COLES I think my moment was – I was called out. The thing about Christmas is, for lots of people, it's really, really tough because there are lots of bereavements at Christmas, because it's that time of year and . . .

FRASER Yes, yes it is.

COLES But I was called out on Christmas Eve to the general hospital, and one of my parishioners had had a very, very premature baby.

FRASER Go on.

COLES I just can't . . . it's pathetic, isn't it?

BOTTLEY No, it's not.

COLES Went to baptize this tiny, tiny, little baby, just fighting for life, and she wasn't allowed to touch the baby but she put her arm into the cot, so the baby's foot rested against her vein, so the pulse of her life . . . Anyway, baptized the baby and he's now a bonny, bonny boy and doing very, very well, but it was just so powerful, so moving.

FRASER There is a thing when you do funerals at Christmas, because there's quite a lot in the run-up, and then when people see the sort of general bonhomie as sort of being an insult to their grief. So, I've known people who've put up all the decorations and then you've gone in and they've torn them down. So, you go in there to talk about somebody's loved one that's died – I have a specific thing in mind here – but in their grief they've torn all – they're only half-torn down. It was just awful about that sort of disjunct between their pain and – and what you wanted to say – this is part of – it's not grumpiness to talk about the problem with the sort of over-sentimentalized because actually it's the people who walked in darkness that have seen a great light . . .

COLES Have seen a great light.

FRASER And, actually, there are so many lights going on that you don't see the light. I mean, I know that's a bit of a cliché, but it's to them that the message exists and yet they pull down the decorations because they thought the message broadly conceived was a sort of insult to their grief.

COLES Have you ever had a punch-up at Midnight Mass in the back . . .

BOTTLEY I've had lots of drunk people, and sometimes the vicar to be fair. [*laughter*] But I think it's traditional, ain't it, that, you know, the pubs open their doors and the church opens its doors and that's what happens. But what the worst thing is, is that when you're looking after multiple churches, if you're in a rural context, sometimes people forget that you've got another church to go to because they're only in their little village. They invite you back for drinks after the carol service. Then they invite you back for drinks after the next carol service. And then, you know, you've got a Midnight Communion, and then you over-consecrate at various other things. And then you've got your home visits as well that you've got to do. So, my top tip for any curates out there is organize taxis for Christmas Eve because by the time you get to Midnight Communion you need to keep that sermon short.

FRASER But it's changed, hasn't it? Because, when the pubs stopped their closing time at sort of 11.30 or something they used to, that was the point you used to get boozed-up people coming out of the pub into the church, because, 'Ooh, why don't we go to the church?' – that was what they'd say after the pub. But now the licensing laws allow the pubs to stay open later and later, you get far fewer pissed people in church.

COLES No, not in Finedon.

BOTTLEY There's one way to combat that, though.

COLES Not in Finedon.

BOTTLEY Serve drinks in church. That's the way to combat it, ain't it? Have a sherry service. The rows over the mulled wine recipe are just, you know, the stuff of legend, aren't they? 'And I do this every year, I do this every year.' You know, and it's just – the fights in the kitchen between mothers' union members are just, you know, the number of times . . .

COLES And it's all about generosity, isn't it? Everyone's supposed to be being at their most generous.

BOTTLEY Yeah, yeah. So, I remember a churchwarden. It was a nativity service for the toddler group, so the idea of getting the under-3s to learn lines was just ridiculous. Let's just dress them up, parade them around: all anybody wants is just the photograph and 'Away in a manger'. Let's just do that, then let's all get out of here alive. And I remember pulling up to church and standing in the car park and the churchwarden coming out and going, 'I wouldn't go in there if I were you.' [*laughter*] And I went, 'Is it that bad?' And he went, 'Yeah . . .'

COLES 'It's not for the likes of you, Vicar.' [*laughter*]

BOTTLEY . . . 'Let's just take a little walk round, shall we?' So, we did. We went for a little walk round, and we went in with about three minutes to spare. And it wasn't the kids, the kids were fine. They didn't mind what they were doing. It's the mums and the dads that were insistent their little sweetheart was going to get their moment in the starlight.

FRASER I've never had that. I've really never had that.

COLES I think another interesting thing, and it's to do with the power of that crib in the patch of light, it's at that

moment we're never more keenly aware that God is equi-
distant from everyone. And at Knightsbridge, where we
used to do these kind of big charity carols – I remember one year, among our readers were the Grand Mufti
and Rod Stewart; you know, it was that sort of thing. But
it was always kind of wonderful because at the end of it
you would have the great and the good and the sort of
Tatler-reading, *Tatler*-photographed people, and then
there would be the street homeless people who were our
population by night. And just for a moment there would
be a sense that we were all the same, equally distant from
God; not this great big warrior, flaming, coming down
from heaven with a sword, but this little baby in a crib.

BOTTLEY Yeah, and as a mum, yourself, you used to look
at those images of Mary holding Jesus and you just – of
course you think what if it was my baby?

FRASER Okay, best Christmas film. Bottley?

BOTTLEY Oh, *Die Hard*, absolutely, without question.
Top three: *Die Hard*, *Muppet Christmas Carol* . . .
number three? It could be . . .

FRASER *Wonderful Life.*

BOTTLEY . . . *Gremlins*, or *It's a Wonderful Life*, ain't it.

COLES I thought you were my friend.

BOTTLEY Come on, it's not Christmas till you've seen Hans
Gruber fall off a Nakatomi building.

FRASER Jingle bell, jingle bell, jingle bell rock – that brilliant bit – and Yippee Ki Yay. Oh, we can't say – we can't
say the rude bit after that.

BOTTLEY It's brilliant, it's a brilliant Christmas movie.

FRASER It's the best Christmas movie.

COLES *It's a Wonderful Life, It's a Wonderful Life* and then *Winter Light* by Ingmar Bergman, about a failed priest in Sweden in the winter. [*laughter*]

BOTTLEY He's so much fun at parties.

FRASER So, this is Christmas: you can go and have Ingmar Bergman with you and then, with your mum, you can go and have the readings on New Year's Eve. What a miserable time. [*laughing*]

COLES Of course, Christmas Day, three o'clock, Queen's Speech. Does the Bottley household stop?

BOTTLEY Only if it's had its dinner and there's nothing else on. It's not a massive tradition, okay. We never watched it growing up. But when I have watched it, yeah, it's been – I mean she always talks about her faith, don't she, so whenever I've watched it, I've always thought, actually, this is a better sermon than I preached this morning, you know.

COLES Exactly. I think – a couple of years ago she did one and I just thought I don't think I've ever heard the essentials of Christian faith laid out so effectively.

FRASER Everything has to stop in my house, even if you're in the middle of dinner you stop.

BOTTLEY Really?

COLES Because your dad is ex-forces.

FRASER No, I think my mum is a particular driving force of this, but we all have to sit round. And there was a tradition, and we've sort of managed to get rid of it, where you don't open your presents until after you've heard the Queen.

COLES You last that long?

FRASER Yeah, no. There was a tradition that you have to wait for – the Queen sort of gives you permission to – that's all gone now; we even open ours the night before. [laughing]

COLES Downright continental.

FRASER It's continental, exactly.

COLES You'll be having a duvet next. [laughter] But the thing I love about the Queen's speech, it's just one of those moments when you kind of think it's a point around which everybody gathers and hears something.

BOTTLEY It's not. It's just not a thing – it's just not a thing in our house.

COLES Do you think this is an illusion of . . .

BOTTLEY It's never been a thing. I didn't even know there was a Queen's speech until I left home.

FRASER Well, the Bottley lot – I mean, you just do feel . . .

BOTTLEY Are we the only people that are missing out?

FRASER . . . that this is something . . .

COLES But you're not, I suspect you're not.

FRASER No, I think you're probably not. But we had a sense that this was one of those sort of moments where the whole – I felt – the whole nation was listening to Her Majesty the Queen, that everybody was gathered round and we were all brought together by that. And no, no, no,

I understand that it's not the case, but it was extraordinary that . . .

COLES Don't laugh at me, but we used to stand for the National Anthem.

BOTTLEY Did you?

COLES Yeah. We had to. My father, who's ex-forces, he would stand to attention.

BOTTLEY My house was more socialist than I thought it was. Absolutely not. You were still eating your dinner . . .

FRASER What's socialism got to do with it?

COLES The Queen's more socialist than . . . Giles.

Hey listen, one more thing: of course Christmas presents. What do you want in your stocking on Christmas morning, Kate Bottley?

BOTTLEY Someone else to cook the lunch. That would be lovely.

COLES So, a chef.

BOTTLEY Yeah, that would be really nice.

COLES Giles?

FRASER I don't need presents, I've got everything I need. Seriously, I don't really need presents. And I love the cooking, oh I absolutely love the cooking. I love it and I'm a fascist in the kitchen; I absolutely – I want to do it, don't touch it, I've got to make everything happen. That I love, really love that.

COLES Could I just ask why no one has asked me what I want in my stocking?

FRASER What do you want in your stocking? What do you want – what shall we get you?

BOTTLEY What do you want in your stocking?

COLES I don't want anything. I just want everyone to be happy. But if I could have something, I'd quite like the Crown Jewels.

FRASER Is that a euphemism for something rude? [*laughter*]

BOTTLEY You keep your private life to yourself, Colesy.

COLES Well, on that note, if any of us want to have a licence to be able to serve Christmases in the future, we'd better bail out.

[*music*]

Can I just say, before we do that, to you both, very happy Christmas.

FRASER And to you, old boy.

BOTTLEY Also with you.

[*clapping*]

Music: 'Away in a manger' sung by a cathedral choir

Easter

Broadcast on Easter Day 2020, at 1.30 p.m.

Presenters: RICHARD COLES
                  KATE BOTTLEY
                  GILES FRASER

Producer: NEIL MORROW

Series editor: CHRISTINE MORGAN

Music: 'Two Easter Sunday Sweethearts' by Jimmy Boyd

COLES Easter: the church full, loud with song, fragrant with flowers, children scampering round the churchyard looking for chocolate eggs. Well, not this year, surely the weirdest Easter in our careers. Churches locked, congregations at home, the tech savvy among the clergy live streaming services from the dining room, the less tech savvy flooding Facebook with close-ups of their nasal hair (mea culpa). Fortunately, Kate Bottley and Giles Fraser are savvy enough to meet today via our laptops to finish our series of *Three Vicars* conversations with the greatest day of all.

Kate – Easter, the greatest day of all, but surely the weirdest one that you've ever known.

BOTTLEY It's – it's a bizarre Easter; it doesn't feel like the ramp-up that it usually has. It's really hard to find the light in the darkness at the moment. And the journey towards Easter Day, it doesn't – I don't feel like popping champagne corks like I usually do.

COLES Don't you find also the differentiation of the day, of the week, of the church season has kind of vanished? I mean, I'm sometimes – I put my pyjamas on at half past three the other day and got a little bit sketchy with compline, and that never happens.

BOTTLEY We didn't get up till four o'clock the other day, and Graham looked at the clock and went, 'Is it already six o'clock?' And I said, 'Yeah, because we've only been up for two hours.' There's no pattern, there's no rhyme, there's no reason to it; we've turned into perpetual teenagers in our house.

COLES How about you, Giles? Are you like me? You're in a parish church: I guess that has a certain structure, but it's very odd, isn't it?

FRASER Well, the other way of looking at it is it's the most Eastery, certainly the most Lenten Lent, I've ever been through. So, at the beginning of Lent, on Ash Wednesday, I had people here in my church and I marked them all on their heads and told them they're going to die. That's what we do: know that you are dust and to dust you shall return. And at that point, when I did that, no one had died yet, but then people started to die and that whole sort of thing that happens with Lent, with fasting, with withdrawal, with the presence of death, that is so much more real and alive this year than it's ever been for me. So, this isn't about giving up chocolate this year; this is – this felt like the real thing to me.

COLES But the thing is, at the end of Lent – no matter how kind of sketchy or faint our attempts to walk with Jesus Christ the way of the cross – is Easter. That's when we do come together, when we do light the Easter candle, when the church that was dark is suddenly full of light. What's going to happen? Because that isn't going to happen this year. I don't know. I might live stream myself singing the Exultet or something. But it's just this extraordinary sense of being excluded from that assembly in which we kind of know who we are, in which Easter happens. That's the thing that's kind of – I'm finding really weird.

FRASER The most important thing to say, I suppose, is that we light the candle in the darkness, the resurrection. And, you know, when we do bring the candle into church, you have the darkened church and we're always worried: will that candle really illuminate? Is it really enough for us to build our whole faith on, because the resurrection is absolutely everything that our faith is built upon? But we bring it in and we say 'The light of Christ', and those flickers, however sort of – we're worried that they're going to go out; is it really going to light ourselves up? But it does. And there's something so beautiful, even being locked out of church, about this day and about that candle and about the resurrection that it signifies. I think it's just wonderful this year.

COLES And of course that hope is not an abstract thing at all. It comes precisely because it lies on the far side of the cross, which is where we're all destined. Kate, how about you?

BOTTLEY My thoughts are that it's almost like the first Easter, in that it'll go largely unnoticed. There will be a rumour of Easter around, rather than a sort of massive declaration of it. And I think there might be some lessons in there, for me certainly, because I've been thinking about what we'll do as a family, because we're based at home, what our Easter at home will look like and how different that will be from Easters when I was in parish and Easters when I'm broadcasting is that you know that I'm out and about, the family have a snatched Easter from me.

Whereas this year it'll probably be mostly just us, huddled together in a room, with the rumour of the resurrection, which has a lovely echo of the first Easter for me.

COLES Giles?

FRASER Richard, I want to ask you really about this Easter quite a lot because you quite like dressing up, don't you? You like your copes and you like your processions.

COLES Where did you get such an idea? [*laughter*]

BOTTLEY He's still going to be doing it. He's going to be parading around his living room in the full gear, walking the dogs in it – in a full cope.

FRASER This is Easter stripped of all the dressing up and the wandering around that us Anglican clergy are often guilty of confusing with – there's the Protestant bit in me coming out – confusing with the sort of core message of Easter. But now we just have to face it, raw and unadorned, the resurrection.

COLES Well, I'm all for a raw and unadorned resurrection. It's interesting, I was thinking – I was looking at the famous Titian painting of the *Noli me tangere*, when Jesus encounters Mary Magdalen in the garden and he says to her, 'Well, actually, don't cling to me,' and recoils from her. But, of course, now it's just a picture of social distancing to me. [*laughter*] An interesting one.

BOTTLEY Yeah, a woman in Aldi looked at me with the same look of horror the other day, when I went . . .

COLES *Noli me tangere.* For me, what's different about this Easter is that it's my first Easter as a widow and so themes of death and resurrection are just really, really powerful for me now. Lent felt well prepared for because I was already experiencing the toughness of that. Social isolation I was already prepared for because my household has been halved. What it'll look like on Easter Day, when we look to the grave and find it empty because it's given forth the fruit of our salvation, I don't know, but it's certainly going to be different from how it's ever felt before.

FRASER Do you feel angry about it as well, that, I mean, when we talk about resurrection and the fact of David's loss is still so raw with you?

COLES No, I don't feel angry, and I've always known that the fact of resurrection is not something which gives you a 'get out of jail free' card from death; of course it doesn't, it's on the far side of that. It does feel a little bit theoretical, a little bit theological, and at the moment it's not an experience in which I feel much detachment; I'm very much in the middle of it. So, in a way, this Lent has been the most Lenten Lent of all because the way has been hard and narrow and stony and dark. So, I don't know. The different thing – of course, normally we do this together, don't we? We walk that walk with our parishes. We walk that walk with our communities. We walk that walk with the people closest to us, and now I seem to be walking that walk with people via social media, so that everything is different about this Lent and this Easter.

FRASER We had that reading the other day about the raising of Lazarus, and I was really struck in that reading by both Mary and Martha going to Jesus, 'If you'd have been here, he wouldn't have died.' Almost anger in their voice, and I could just feel all those people saying to God, 'If you'd have bloody been here, this wouldn't have happened.' There's a sort of real visceral nature of people's response to this hideous plague and people suffering so much and their anger at that, which is – it's a part of the whole Lenten experience, isn't it?

COLES Yeah, because we don't offer a palliative, we're not here with analgesia for this, we're not here with anaesthetic. People sometimes think, don't they, that Christianity is an attempt to shy away from the hard realities of life, to seek some sort of cheap comfort? It's exactly the opposite, because we stand at the foot of the cross and everything you need to know about just how brutal life can be is there in front of you. And, of course, you feel all that stuff. I find you cannot live in grief permanently because you have to feed the dogs, you have to answer the post, you have to cut your toenails – cutting your toenail in grief, by the way, not great. If you want a stigmata, I can show you stigmata.

I tell you what's odd about it, and maybe this is something interesting in relation to Lent and Easter: grief is not something you do, it's something that happens to you. And you just have to let it happen to you; you're not in control of this at all. And for clergy, because we are so often theoretically in control around bereavement and loss and death and stuff, that's quite an education.

FRASER The other thing, and Kate's brilliant at this, and I find this especially when it's most serious and death is so much present, is the joke. It's just making it funny. And that's one of the things we all, as clergy, when we're together and particularly when, you know, things are dark and difficult, I mean there's some pretty – pretty fruity humour that comes.

BOTTLEY Oh, the darkness of people's humour at the moment is just – it's one of the best things about this whole process. Did you see the fellow clergyman who set himself on fire at evening prayer the other day?

COLES Yeah.

FRASER What?

BOTTLEY Oh just . . . So, he was doing the evening prayer via whatever – Skype, Zoom, whatever, Facebook live, whatever it is he was doing – and he'd got a lit candle behind him and his jumper caught fire; his acrylic polyester mix, or whatever it was, suddenly went up. And he did the most British response and he went, 'Oh dear, I appear to be alight.' And it was just – and he sort of, like, patted himself out and then kind of carried on with the psalm or whatever he was doing. It was just – it was just lovely.

But this is so refreshing because one of my great frustrations in this process – you know, obviously I am in with my family in a lovely sized house, there's a lot to be cheerful about. You know, we're doing all right but when it gets tough I've wanted to throw rainbow – you know the rainbow pictures that are in our windows – I wanted to rip them up. And I've wanted to extinguish the candles. This kind of perpetual cheerfulness. And if you actually ask anybody how they are, and then you go, 'Do you know, I'm having a really rubbish day today, I feel awful,' and they go, 'Well, chin up.' You know, and I just – grrrhh. The place for lament for me has been the big question. Where's this place for going 'This is awful. I am having a miserable time'? And if you express that at the moment, in any way, shape or form, especially wearing one of these, it seems to be like, 'Come on, buck up, you know you can do this.' And I just – where's the place for me feeling a bit sorry for meself?

COLES I saw a great cartoon the other day on the internet, and it was someone with a sign saying, 'Let's beat coronavirus. Free hugs'! [*laughter*]

One of the things I've learnt, especially since David died, is that my illusion of omnipotent competence as a clergyman, which was always pretty fragile, has completely crumbled, because I'm simply not capable. I can't be detached, I can't be without emotion, I can't always cope. And the parish has been fantastic at exercising its priestly ministry to me, rather than me exercising my priestly ministry to them.

FRASER It's particularly hard to learn how to be given to, isn't it? When you're the person who's used to being, in some sense, a provider and you find your worth from being a provider to, as it were, to be a recipient of people's love and to depend upon people's love for your own well-being.

COLES And to know that we are also carrying our own crosses, aren't we? We also have our burdens, we're also wounded and scarred, and that makes us less than the best we can be. And people understand it and cope with it and bear with it. That's Easter.

FRASER I sit in the church and just cry sometimes. I don't do much really.

COLES I sit in church and cry when we get the gas bill. [*laughter*]

BOTTLEY I sit in church and cry when there's preaching going on.

FRASER Bad preaching?

BOTTLEY Bad preaching going on.

COLES But, Kate, what's it like for you not having a regular attachment to a parish church, not being the person who has to organize the Stations of the Cross or, I don't know, bang your Lenten tambourine, whatever you do in your own tradition?

BOTTLEY [*laughing*] Yes, those flags are going unwaved, Richard. I feel redundant. So, somebody said to me, 'Oh, you must be very busy supporting your community at the moment.' I thought, I'm not. I've been laid in bed eating chocolate most of the day. You know, so there's that redundancy of not feeling very useful at all, not making a blind bit of difference. I mean, I've knocked on the neighbours' doors. Sandra, three doors down, she

wanted some eggs, so I did that. But you feel totally redundant in this. A funeral came in for me last week and
they needed some funeral cover, and I suddenly got in
this awful panic that I didn't know how to do funerals
any more, because it's been so long now since I did one,
because of the way things are, that I just felt totally
redundant.

COLES I thought the hokey cokey worked really well.

BOTTLEY [*laughing*] But there's this thing, I was on air on
Sunday morning and on Saturday night I had this over-
whelming feeling of trying to be some sort of national
cheerleader, and I just thought, I can't do that, I don't feel
very cheerful at all. And actually that suddenly occurred
to me, that when we stand at that communion table and
we feel totally ill equipped for what we're about to do,
it's actually just the same, it's just in a different place,
that I went live on Sunday morning and went, 'Morning.
This is *Good Morning Sunday* on BBC Radio 2', and
I thought, I don't feel this, I'm not feeling this, so I'm just
going to have to fake it until I make it. And I think that's
part of priestly ministry too, isn't it?

COLES We are, in a way, the Red Coats, aren't we? A spiritual kind of community Red Coats. Sounds slightly dis-
paraging but I think it's an important thing to do, is that
we are there to provide leads or focuses or organization.
One of the things I've always thought of being a vicar of
a parish like mine, which is a small country parish, is
my job is just to lightly organize the natural goodness

of people. And that's been fantastic. The community response to what's happening at the moment has been really, really great; people are coming together, making sure that those who are at the edges, the very margins of our community, are looked after. And it's also something that's a very interesting thing: it's not very religious, in a way, and that I feel – it's a classic Anglican model, isn't it? – we exist for the benefit of our non-members. Most of the good stuff that's happening in our parish is happening with people of different faiths, of no faiths, just that natural goodness, you know, encouraging it. Giles?

FRASER Well, I'm not as biddable as you two, or as nice, and I think I'm also not quite as community focused or facing as you. And I suddenly realized that when I'm in an empty church and pray in an empty church, that there's the one side of the Anglican vicar, which is towards the congregation, and there's the other side, which is God-facing. And I find myself more and more thinking about my role as being the God-facing-ness of this, which, I mean, when you turn round and you do backward facing, and you're facing the cross and you're facing the altar and you have your back to the congregation – not that there's any congregation there – it feels a different sort of way of being a priest. So, we are strong between those two things, aren't we?

COLES Michael Ramsey called it in that book about the Christian priest today, using language of the time, he said, 'We're on the manward side of God and the

Godward side of man.' And it is true, this strange Janus-like existence of facing both directions at once.

FRASER Yeah.

BOTTLEY And that maintenance of our public and private faces, it's trickier than ever at the moment because there's that sort of, you know, you dog collar up or you get doing your thing, and you sort of have to pull yourself up by your own bootstraps. I wonder what Easter morning will feel like when that might be in my home. Will I still be able to put as good a face on it for those people that I love most in the world?

COLES One thing I've found, actually – and I got a sort of taste of this when I was in a monastery for two years – is that I've been offering the Eucharist at home. I've set up at home in line with the archbishops' and the bishops' instructions and I'm saying it on my own, like a monk would have done at a side altar in the Middle Ages. And actually, funnily enough, I've felt much more connected to the universal Church doing that than I've been perhaps in a parish setting.

FRASER There is something rather beautiful about the Zoom Eucharists that we've been doing, which sounds crackers really but you see everybody on the screen and people sit in their own homes and read . . .

COLES What about some technicals? I got a delivery this morning of palm crosses, two hundred and fifty palm crosses, which normally we'd distribute at Palm Sunday, which is, of course, the beginning of Holy Week, and next Sunday. Now I'm working out ways of delivering through sanitized bags and using our community delivery system at the moment. It's a very odd feeling that, isn't it? That we can't all gather, do our procession around the church. Palm Sunday was the day I started my ministry in Finedon ten years ago, so it's a significant anniversary.

BOTTLEY There's a lot of redundant donkeys this year, isn't there? [*laughter*] They're having a kind of a bit of a rest. It's nice for them, it's nice for them to have a break, ain't it?

COLES Let's hope it's just a break.

BOTTLEY Do you think they'll be able to claim their eighty per cent off the government for their fee, the donkeys?

COLES I think, as well, there's something – I've always felt this – that Palm Sunday has a sort of phoney war feeling about it, that this is something that feels kind of slightly kind of over-excitable. And actually it's going somewhere bad. The first week of lockdown felt a bit phoney war to me, too; there was a sort of strange resonance between those two experiences there. Because we know that it's going to get much tougher over the next few weeks, just as on Palm Sunday we know that Good Friday lies ahead. So, there is this kind of sense of the world coinciding with the church calendar in a new way.

FRASER I did it in Jerusalem a few years ago, and walking down the Mount of Olives and going into the city of Jerusalem, surrounded by soldiers, with a sense of tension and also, I have to say, with huge irritation at the other clergy all dressing up and poncing about, which just really wound me up. But there was a real sense that the religious and the political met each other, in a way that felt, you know, similar to how it might well have felt in Jesus' day with the politics and the religion feeling very, sort of, interconnected.

BOTTLEY My experience of Jerusalem at Easter was – I was filming a documentary for the BBC a couple of years ago, *In the Footsteps of Judas*. We went to the Church of the Holy Sepulchre. Well, it was like a bun fight, you know. You've got all these, kind of, guards and people holding each other back, and the queue's round the block; and you've got, you know, today's the day for the Greek Orthodox to have the shrine and tomorrow's the day for the Ethiopians to have the – and whatever – but it's like a cattle market. And then I became aware that they were holding all these crowds back for me, for me to go and do my bit of filming that I'd got to do. So, we got to the place where the tomb is – you've been, you know what it's like. That day was the day for the Greek Orthodox to have the shrine in the Holy Sepulchre. And I can speak a little bit of Greek – a bit more than just 'Can I have, you know, some souvlaki and two beers' – so I had a word with the priest that was stood there . . . you know, sort of 'Yasou, Papas' [*phon.*], and all this sort of stuff, and he sort of pointed into the shrine. And it's, like, for want of a better phrase, it's like a cubicle, is how I would describe it. It's this kind of shed-like thing in the middle of the church, and this is where Jesus' body lay. This is the place where the resurrection happened. And he let me in. And normally you're sort of shovelled through like some sort of queue at Alton Towers, but I found myself in there, in this place, this holiest of places, and he shut the doors behind me. So, all of a sudden, I was completely alone in this place where my faith is founded, where everything that I hold all my belief on is grounded and born from. And it was the most surreal experience I think I've ever had. Utterly silent, utterly connected, utterly joyful but completely terrifying all at the same time; it was everything that I expected the moment of resurrection to feel like – joyful terror, I think is what best describes it.

COLES I think that's very interesting because there are elements in the story that are coming up as we enter Holy Week and the culminating events. For instance, the watch on Maundy Thursday: I think that's going to be a very resonant one. Because I'm doing a watch every day, I'm sitting there – people saying to me the people they wish to pray for. We've had deaths in the parish, of course. We've got, I think, more to come. And so, to sit on my own, with the Blessed Sacrament here at home, praying the prayers of the faithful, all of a sudden that part of the story, when Jesus and the disciples are in Gethsemane. It's so often the way, isn't it? We've been doing this for years and years, we've got decades of experience of doing this, and sometimes the world is such . . . out of joint or surprising, that elements of those stories all of a sudden become foreground.

BOTTLEY But that's exactly what it should be. The world should be forming our traditions. It's not that we impose this. That we reflect what's actually happening. And so, for me, it's really exciting, because we don't know what this is going to look like. I've been so excited thinking about the reflections and the writings that's going to come out of this, and the things to read after this is all done, about what we've actually learnt. How different will we be after this Easter is done? What will our faith then look like after this year? We've got no idea. Some people are saying that the churches are going to be full when this is over. Some people are saying they're going to be empty. One thing's for certain is we can't be the same, not as a nation, not as a faith.

FRASER I mean, who knows? And who knows what the Church will be after this? Kate's right – will people come back? Will they discover they've got better things to do on Sunday mornings? Will our elderly congregation? How many of them will survive? I really worry about my elderly congregation. This virus is particularly acute in this area where I minister in South London. I don't know what's going to happen. I really worry about my church, and I worry about the future of it.

COLES I mean, for example, if we're going to – the likeli-hood is – lose a number of our older, most faithful, most committed members who will die and take with them that commitment, which is not just about being faithfully in church Sunday by Sunday, it's about the standing order, it's about the gift aid, that's going to give us a new reality to live in which I think is going to be very tough indeed. And the austerity and fasting of Lent might extend way beyond the season.

FRASER The challenge is real to the Church, which is, can the Church live by the good news of the resurrection alone? And can we be sustained by what we proclaim today, unsupported by anything else? And that's the nature of faith. And that would be really quite a challenge.

COLES And also, what could be more powerfully an expression of Easter than the discovery of the new life, unimaginable, immeasurable, that lies beyond the fact of our death?

FRASER Yeah.

COLES There's something about that which seems to me to be enormously exciting.

BOTTLEY Because that's the cornerstone of our faith, isn't it? That we believe that if something dies it will be resurrected, it will still bear the scars of its death, it'll still be recognizable, but at the same time completely transformed. So, it's exciting. The thought that the Church might sort of die through this, isn't that what we kind of strive for? Isn't that what we believe in? That through death comes resurrection and transformation?

FRASER Exactly that.

COLES And isn't that perhaps what we're really being called to do, to surrender ourselves to this new and very stark reality and only then will the possibility of that new life, that transformed life, emerge? It's a very tough sermon to preach, that one, isn't it? It's a very tough conversation to have with our colleagues.

FRASER There is real hope in this. I mean, hope is a really interesting word in these times. Hope also means defiance. There's a bloody-mindedness about hope in the times of this virus, which is we will not give in, we will not be defeated, we will celebrate, we will joke, you know, there's – that hope has a number of different moods at this time.

BOTTLEY And there's been a reframing of what we hope for as well. I'm thinking – this is a really trite example, but I found a roast chicken in Aldi, because we couldn't find any chicken, and I found some chicken and I brought it home and there was much rejoicing in the Bottley household in the kitchen, dancing round the kitchen because we were going to have chicken for tea. And two weeks ago that was unthinkable, that was an unthinkable concept. If you'd told me that that would be what we were rejoicing about in our household – affluent, relatively middle-class, well-provided-for household rejoicing at the sight of a roast chicken! There's something in that that I really want to hold on to after this is all done, where there's a new perspective on what brings joy and what brings hope, that I want to never take for granted in the same way that I have done.

FRASER That's completely right, Kate; I totally share that. I had the same experience with a tomato [*laughing*] just the other day. So, there's potential in all of this for renewal, isn't there? I mean, not just for the renewal of the Church – and we talked a little bit about that – but for, strange as it may sound, renewal in society. I mean these things are often pointers to what matters most. You know, when you're in this sort of horrible crisis you – isn't this right? – you sort of huggle, want to hug your loved ones more closely. It shows you the sort of value of the really simple things, like the food that we provide for each other, the care that we have, and all the trivial stuff burns away in this sort of crisis.

COLES One of the things I've discovered in grief is that one of the things that comes with that is this extraordinarily focused perspective; all of a sudden you see stuff in a way you haven't seen it before. You see what's important, you see what's not important, you see your own kind of self-promoting stratagems to get your own way through life. They sort of fade away, and what you just really see is the stuff that really matters, that connects you to people and that disconnects you from people. And only then, when you know the fast and the feast of that, I think, can you understand what that promise of new life really means and how that is sustained by the hope which implants itself into our lives in spite of everything.

I was at David's grave the other day. We were planning to meet there with his family, as a sort of – you know, like a yahrzeit in Jewish tradition, just to gather at the grave and remember him. And we couldn't do it because of this lockdown. And I went there on my bike and I stood there on my own, and it was wonderful; it was terrible and wonderful at the same time, in a way that was utterly paradoxical, and it was, I don't know, I can't describe it . . .

FRASER No.

[*silence*]

COLES That was a conversation killer, wasn't it?

FRASER No, it wasn't a conversation killer . . .

BOTTLEY I'm just having a little cry.

FRASER By the way, that wasn't the silence of 'I don't know what to say' – and there's a lot of this going on. That was the silence of 'That was a very beautiful thing that you just said', and it needed a little bit of space and respect.

COLES Yeah. And then all of a sudden there was me, the Red Coat, jumping in with a gag – mea culpa.

FRASER Yeah, yeah. No. But that's what we do. That's the tension, isn't it? I don't know if we can sustain that level of intensity all the time – so it has to be broken and we have to laugh at it.

[*music, faint strains*]

COLES I love that thing in one of the most beautiful, I think, pieces of liturgy around death and funerals. It's the

Russian Kontakion. We used to sing it in the monastery whenever one of the monks died. It's a very beautiful piece, and then at the end it says, 'And weeping we make our song o'er the grave: Alleluia, alleluia, alleluia.' And that's the paradox, isn't it? We're at the grave, we weep, we've lost, we're destroyed, but. Alleluia, alleluia, alleluia. Dawn is breaking, the light of Christ. Thanks be to God. He is risen.

BOTTLEY He is risen indeed, alleluia.

[*in tears*]

FRASER He is risen indeed. Happy Easter, my loves.

COLES Happy Easter.

BOTTLEY Happy Easter.

Music: 'The Russian Kontakion of the Departed'

WE HAVE A VISION OF A WORLD IN WHICH EVERYONE IS TRANSFORMED BY CHRISTIAN KNOWLEDGE

As well as being an award-winning publisher, SPCK is the oldest Anglican mission agency in the world.

Our mission is to lead the way in creating books and resources that help everyone to make sense of faith.

Will you partner with us to put good books into the hands of prisoners, great assemblies in front of schoolchildren and reach out to people who have not yet been touched by the Christian faith?

To donate, please visit www.spckpublishing.co.uk/donate or call our friendly fundraising team on 020 7592 3900.